So a Com
Walks Into a

So a Comedian Walks Into a Church...

Confessions of a Kneel-Down Stand-Up

Paul Kerensa

DARTON·LONGMAN+TODD

For Zoë,
who has lovingly proofread the entire
book except this page,
so let's hope there are no mistaks.

First published in 2013 by
Darton, Longman and Todd Ltd
1 Spencer Court
140 – 142 Wandsworth High Street
London SW18 4JJ

ISBN 978-0-232-52979-1

A catalogue record for this book is available from the British Library.
Printed and bound in Great Britain by Bell & Bain, Glasgow.

Contents

A Little Foreword

Excuse me for being a little foreword.

Good, now that's out of the way. Welcome to the book. If you're still in the shop, I'd just buy the thing if I were you – it's a real page-turner. If you're browsing for free on the internet – it's a real page-swiper. I'd still buy the print copy. E-readers are all very well, but you can't slam a fly in it, can you?

My name's Paul. What's your name? Why not write it here?

Excellent, now you have to buy it. So now we're introduced. I'm a stand-up comedian, and I'm also a Christian. No, come back ...

I'm on the road a lot. Every Saturday night I'm at another far-flung comedy club. I have never seen this show they call *Strictly Come Dancing*. Ours is the path less travelled, except it's travelled a lot, because it's normally the M1.

The next day, I'll wake up in a yet another spare room or soulless budget hotel; Sunday isn't Sunday unless I can see a tiny kettle. If I want to go to church – and I do – I just find a building with a cross on top and wander in. I've only mistakenly picked a pharmacy on one or two occasions.

So this is a tale of two circuits: of comedy clubs and churches. That, in a nutshell, is what follows.

I've had heckles in Eccles and stage deaths in Caithness; we'll visit the lot. We'll be cheered and booed, and encounter loudmouths and dodgy promoters. We'll do a lot of driving, face a bunch of onstage dilemmas and maybe even appear on telly. And the morning after the night before, we'll meet vicars and pastors, Methodists and Catholics, Baptists, Quakers, candlestick-makers ...

I realise that the likelihood of you, dear reader, being interested in punchlines *and* praise is highly unlikely, but that's okay. All you need to know is that I bestride both. If you're a comedy fan, there's plenty for you here about the world of stand-up and the reality of life on permanent tour. If you're more church-inclined, there's an ecclesiastical smorgasbord.

When at home on a Sunday, the 'norm' for me is a growing Anglican church: traditional in some ways, trying new things in others, and offering a bunch of things to the community – and that's how I like it. On the road, I like to cast the net wide and find something different.

I can only write what I know, so if you're hoping to read about a side of comedy or Christianity that I've left out, apologies. I simply haven't been to an Eastern Orthodox or a New Monastic community. Equally I can't tell you about doing *Live At The Apollo* or a corporate for MI5 – although I can't tell you about that for different reasons.

I've written for TV, radio and stage, but this is the first time of book writing. If any of you know any reason why any of the words should not be joined together, you are not to declare it, please. If you're a churchgoer and anything feels a little close to home, I hope I'm fair to you. If you're a comedian and you think you recognise yourself, it's probably someone else. Some names have been changed and occasionally I've contracted time or altered a placename – please forgive this.

A big thank you to David Moloney and all at DLT, and Nick Ranceford-Hadley and all at Noel Gay, for literally making this happen – without you, this book wouldn't be a book, but scrawled on a toilet wall somewhere. (There are a lot of stories about toilets in this book – I'm sorry for that and don't really know why.)

Gigantic thanks to my parents Di & Rog, and to Mark & Katie, John & Sue and James & Tabitha – your support in countless ways has made this possible.

Kudos too to the many friends who've read a chapter or talked it over: Liz Robinson, Henry Martin, Mark Woodward, Jon Sandys, Jon Holloway, Nick S, Eileen Collins, Tony Vino, Andy Kind, Russ Anderson, Iszi Lawrence, Jez and Jude Gibson, Andrew, David and Jenny Kember ... and anyone else that knows me. A big thank you too if you completed my online survey about churches – your help was invaluable.

Thanks too to the hundreds of comics, comedy-goers and congregants that feature in this book. Without you, I'd be alone in a big room. That happens in at least one chapter and it's awful.

And to Zoë and Joseph and someone I won't name for practical reasons: you're stars, and the reason it's a joy to hit 'Home' on the satnav.

I'll also thank God, because He's my co-writer, and so far hasn't asked for a penny in royalties.

I

Scot Free

Chortling with the Church of Scotland

'Excuse me? Where's the nearest Church of England church?'

'England,' the Scottish woman inevitably replied.

The tourist information helper was an elderly lady who looked like she could be anyone's grandmother, yet also handy in a fight. You could tell that her grey was formally ginger, in common with so many other locals.

As a fellow Celt (Cornish) and redhead (strawberry brunette), I feel a kinsmanship with the Scots, whether they like it or not. Even as I boarded the flight at 'London' Stansted, I could tell I was among friends. I say 'friends' – there were surly looks from a couple of ginger giants certainly, and maybe I spent too long staring at one redhead family.

I say 'London' Stansted too, because it really should be in inverted commas. Living between Gatwick and Heathrow, either 'London' airport would have been ideal, but no, the gig promoter booked me into Stansted, a mere hundred miles away from my house. I wouldn't mind (well, I would) but at the other end I landed in 'Glasgow' Prestwick, an airport that also suffers from Stansted syndrome, being a good hour from the city it represents. Door to door, it would have been about as quick to drive, cycle or pogo stick. The entire trip involved 150 road miles and 250 air miles.

Given the choice, I'd have taken the train. It's better for the environment, and my sanity. Of course my false impression of a rail journey to Scotland is of an old-fashioned smoky platform, where I take the overnight sleeper, sharing my cabin with a wistful world traveller and raconteur. We compare Panama hats and make bets that we can't circumvent the globe in a hot air balloon, until we join a Belgian detective for cocktails and arsenic in the dining car. In truth, it involves four changes and a traipse across the London Underground with luggage before I even board the train. This is followed by a six-hour journey panicking that I'm sitting in someone else's seat because there's a big bloke in the one I've booked, all for a mere two hundred pounds.

The choice was out of my hands – I was furnished with an e-ticket for the plane as soon as the gig was diarised, so I easily jetted from Cambridge Stansted to Ayr Prestwick for a weekend of entertaining stags, hens and a few couples who'd misbooked. Friday and Saturday were planned out; I just had Sunday morning to plan.

Yes, I'm the one person who reads those guides in hotels and flicks to the back for the list of local churches. Typically, my hotel didn't have one, but I thought the tourist information centre might help get me my God fix. I rephrased the question of course – asking for any kind of fix in Glasgow city centre can introduce you to some unsavoury characters. I was already in danger of crossing this good woman by forgetting that Church of England may not be so common when not in England.

'You'll be wanting Church of Scotland,' she said kindly. It didn't sound that kind, but given the idiocy of my previous two questions, anything but a head-butt could be considered kind.[1]

I'm not clued up on the difference between Churches of England and Scotland, so presumed it just meant shortbread and Irn Bru for communion.

'And I'd find one ...?'

'Right on Renfrew Street, left on Renfield Street, right on Renferren Street ...'

I needed to retain this information till Sunday morning. It lasted all of three seconds before exiting my brain. I thought to ask her again but she gave me a look that said, 'Get lost'. So I headed back to the hotel and got lost.

This venue could be a tough gig, often with large parties and big celebrations. I love a party blower as much as the next man, but the bigger the group, the higher the ratio of 'people who haven't really come along for the comedy' versus 'the person who booked it'. They can be tricky.[2]

Friday night was lovely though – the stags and hens were on good form, and there were a few work parties who all seemed to have achieved the impossible: leaving the office joker at home, or telling him

---

[1] My irrational fear of Scottish head-butts can be blamed on Russ Abbot c.1987.
[2] Especially if you start talking about ratios.

the event was somewhere else.[3] The other comics were a joy to be with, everyone had a nice gig, and we all patted each other on the back on a job well done, and by 'job' I mean, 'twenty minutes of talking at people'.

Saturday's show was different: full of large single-sex parties and a big footie match that meant drinking from noon.

Call-time came, as did stag do after stag do after hen do,[4] in all their shapes and sizes ...

A rough guide to rough stag and hen parties

- **The Shameless Fancy-Dress Brigade:** Six foot six and bold as brass, dressed as Scooby Doo, marching through the streets of Glasgow. They've been drinking since Thursday and they lost the groom-to-be about a day ago.
- **The Geeky Stag Do:** The cutest of pre-marriage revellers. Most wear glasses, and the ones who don't keep bumping into things.
- **The Underattended Hen Do**: Four of them, still in work clothes. Someone has planned this particularly badly.
- **The Learner Plates**: Found attached to any hen. Sometimes if they're having a post-wedding hen party, they're P-plates. In either case, their behaviour normally means they need their licence revoked.
- **Angels and Demons**: If more than one hen party is gathered, the odds are that you'll see one lot with angel wings and the other with devil horns, as if the dress code was 'spiritual warfare'. It's a glimpse of the end days, only with more high heels and sambuca.
- **Overweight Superheroes:** Always a favourite with men of a certain age. If at the same event as the tottering angels and devils, it's a glimpse of Armageddon with a chubby Bananaman come to save the day.

---

[3] It's always a 'him'.
[4] i.e. There were two stag dos after one hen do.

As the audience passed us on the way to falling into their seats, even the non-religious comedians started praying for a show like last night's. We paced the floor, and we paced the Red Bulls.

Bombastic intro music blared out of the speakers and woke up two drunk Spider-Men. The compère walked out to the baying mob, and spent a few minutes trying to get them to notice he was there. As I was the first act on, I keenly watched both compère and audience for any hint as to how to play this: any glints of fun folks in the audience we could chat to or lightly rib. Any chance they might warm to a one-liner or two, or a rant, or a spot of wry satire about the government's attitude to public sector pensions.

After ten minutes of making them cheer, the compère put the microphone back in the stand: amber light to a comedian. Any second now he'd say my name and 'The Power of Love' by Huey Lewis and the News would play (my choice of intro – it gives the audience a sense that they're about to get upbeat, cheesy, middle-class nonsense).

'… Please welcome Paul Kerensa!' and 'Gold Digger' by Kanye West played.

Now, I'm not blaming the entire stage death on that one technical hiccup, but perhaps if their expectations had been more in-line with what I was going to do, the show might have gone better. I don't do any jokes about life in the hood. I live in Guildford. We haven't got a ghetto. We occasionally have a gateau, but Waitrose runs out of stock so quickly.

It wasn't a death – just a minor injury. Some jokes were hitting home, but so were some audience heckles. Generally the set consisted of me trying to get them onside by playing the ginger card. 'I'm one of you!' was the theme, even if my accent gave away that I very much was not, and as we've already established, I'm strawberry brunette.

The crucial rule for lairy gigs is to never leave too long a pause. I did once (to breathe) and a loud heckle came from nowhere – well not nowhere, right at the back near the toilets. Because it was right at the back, and the general hubbub of four hundred people wasn't too quiet, I couldn't pick out any of what was said. It didn't help that it was in strong and slurring Glaswegian.

'What's that?' I asked to get a second hearing.

The sentence was repeated, which is more than I can do here. It's in no way intended as a slight on the people of Glasgow – it's my soft Cornish ears that are at fault. I'm from the other end of this land mass.

We're not *meant* to be able to communicate. The Tower of Babel: it's in the Bible. So no offence to the many lovely and often quite comprehensible Glaswegians, but if this man sounded drunk and aggressive to me, it may have been because he was drunk and aggressive.

I panicked. What joke did I have in my arsenal ready for this? I needed a putdown, and fast. Show who's boss, which I think was meant to be me, although all evidence indicated otherwise. So – and I'm not proud of this – my response to his heckle was an unrepeatable sentence that implied I knew of his mum.

The whole room fell silent. I had silenced him! It had worked! But I had silenced *everyone*. Especially my conscience, who just gave an internal, 'uh oh', followed by the sound of a closing door and a flushing noise.

'All he said,' came a soft Edinburgh voice from the front row, 'was that he's ginger too.'

Whoops. I'd just started a fight for no real reason. He was merely commenting on the fact that as a ginger man, I wanted to feel connected to this audience, and he was reaching out – one redhead to another reddishhead. I had shunned his metaphorical outreached hand, and instead upped the ante.

'You're ginger too?' I blustered. 'Ah. Well, what I just said about your ... I'm sure very lovely mother ... At least it would explain why you're ginger too.'

I'd nearly got away with it, until a different heckler pointed out, 'You're not even that ginger,' followed by the audience breaking into small groups to discuss just how not ginger I was, as well as drinks orders and how bad the football was today.

I made it to the end, using the compère's technique of making them cheer to ensure I left the stage to applause ('A round of applause for our fine ginger friend at the back! ...Bye!'), and made my way to the green room, red in face if not in hair. The other comedians were a mix of supportive and brazen about the fact that they hadn't seen the act because their food had arrived. The nagging thought remained that I'd stopped being *me* onstage tonight, albeit briefly. There's no harm in dropping the script for some light banter, but when you stop doing what you want to do onstage – and what I want to do is tell jokes and make people have a nice time – then you start to question the act.

Annoyed with myself, and a little ashamed, I decided I deserved nothing more than to go back to the hotel room, via the bar, and maybe the cinema.

*   *   *

I should have got a map. I'm walking through the streets of Glasgow looking for the church in Renfrew Road, or was it Renfield? My inability to listen has caused me to needlessly offend a well-meaning heckler with words I generally don't use onstage, and has now caused me to become lost. I'd ask a stranger for directions, but there aren't many about at ten o'clock on a Sunday morning, and even if there were, I'm afraid my ears will land me in hot water.

Last night's gig is reverberating around my skull. Onstage you present a persona – it's not necessarily *you* but it is a version of *you*. I'm not an aggressive man. I try to be nice. Yet last night was one of those gigs where I decided to play the audience at their own game, and actually found the hecklers to be far nicer than I was. I don't like what this says about me. I'm hoping it just says, 'I misinterpreted a Glaswegian accent'. Yet I can't help but think of the Liverpudlian priest who once said to me post-show, 'It's nice to see a comedian who doesn't think you need to be vulgar to be funny.' If he had been at the gig last night, I'd have wondered what he'd make of it, and why he'd come all the way from Liverpool.

I walk, lost. I'm just about to give up and retrace my steps when I see a sign. Not a heavenly sign as such, but a street name: Renfrew Street. This was one of the names the tourist information lady mentioned! Probably! And look! There's a lovely family of five redheads all dressed up nice, turning left onto Renfield Street.

I follow them, and sure enough they walk right into the McDonald's next door to a small church. I leave them to it and wander into the Tardis-like building: traditional and wee on the outside, but ultra-modern white walls and funky chairs on the inside.

'You're most welcome. Do take a seat anywhere,' a sidesman says.[5]

There's a huge bookshop at the back. Not just a mobile trolley with a few dog-eared copies of *The Purpose Driven Life*. This is like a mini Waterstones. There are commentaries on every book in the Bible,

---

[5] If the old kids' game is to be believed, he should have said, 'Sidesman says take a seat,' before I obeyed him.

sections on Mission, Church History, Hermeneutics, Epistemology, Semiotics and several other words that I've vaguely heard of. I always thought Hermeneutics was the session at our sports centre between Zumba and Bodypump.

The worship band strikes up, and sounds more like an orchestra. Not only drums, guitars and keyboard, but we also have a cellist and a fiddler. It means the opening music has a truly Celtic feel to it. I'm slow to sing along – it sounds that beautiful – but when we move into 'Amazing Grace', you can't help but get swept up in the moment. The strings section, the location, the fact that I can hear the Scottish accent in the congregation's singing, all make this the finest version of John Newton's great song that I've ever heard or had the joy of singing. I have visions of Welsh churches at the same moment belting out 'Bread of Heaven', Irish churches giving it 'Danny Boy' and English churches muttering something about an 'English Country Garden'.

The musical worship gives way to the welcome, and I half-want the cello and violin to continue under the whole service, like the backing for a Visit Scotland commercial. Instead the dulcet Hibernian tones of the minister greet us. This is an accent I could listen to for hours, and nearly do, as church news and banns of marriage alone last for fifteen minutes. But it's Glasgow city centre, and there's a lot going on. Fair play to them.

The reading is from Ephesians 5: 'Wives, be subordinate to your husbands as to the Lord.' Controversial, and not often preached upon. I presume we'll get a nice placatory explanation of how actually you *can* read it to mean we're all equal. I presume wrong. Most would focus on the later verse instructing husbands to love their wives as Christ loves the church. Not this guy. We're not in a C of E now. This is C of S. There's no watering down of wine or sermons here.

Still intoning as the vocal equivalent of hot chocolate, the minister proceeds to tell us how women *should* promise to obey their husbands. No room for ambiguity here. My, does it get uncomfortable, especially for the couples who've just had their banns read. The minister marrying them may not give them the vow-flexibility they had hoped for.

The minister encourages that during our time of prayer, we consider the challenges of what's been said, only looking at women as he says so. Wow, they've been given homework.

As we bow our heads though, my focus is on last night's gig. It is challenging being a comedian who's a Christian,[6] and sometimes you win, sometimes you lose. I like to think I'm an example of human loveliness when I'm onstage. Last night I was an example of how to needlessly start a pub brawl.

Closing worship is a chance for me to reflect. As another holy concert plays, courtesy of the string section, I resolve to try and be more 'me' onstage and less what the audience expects from a comedian. I resolve to accept when a gig is getting out of hand and that, sometimes, I'm powerless to turn it. I resolve to put it behind me and just be glad that, for all I know, there were no priests there. And I resolve to listen to more folk music (it really is a lovely violin).

The inevitable invitation comes: 'Do stay for coffee.' It's practically part of the blessing in churches nowadays. You can roll it straight into, 'In the name of the Father, the Son, and the Holy Spirit …'. I wouldn't be surprised to find that in the 1665 prayer book there's a section of alternative invitations:

The minister says:
Do join us for coffee.
or
You're welcome to stay for coffee.
or on festival days
Do stay for coffee and biscuits.

The congregation may reply:
Thanks, but I've got to rush off.

The coffee must be good here – there's a big queue. So while it dies down I browse the bookshop, run by an elderly lady so tiny she barely appears above the table of books. I hope she doesn't have the job of stacking the shelves.

'New here or just visiting?'

'Just passing through. I'm working here this weekend.'

'Oh, whereabouts?' she continues, sipping a coffee that she must have fetched during the closing blessing, the wily lass.

I'm not proud of last night's show so I consider lying, saying that I'm

---

[6] … as opposed to a 'Christian comedian', which implies putting on skits at parish away days.

working at Prestwick Airport and taking a trip to far-off Glasgow. But I'm in a church branch of Waterstones, and there are rules against deceit.

'The comedy club up the road.'

'Oh, Matt and Emily went there last night,' she says, and I gulp. I blink and she's gone to fetch them.

Uh oh. Perhaps no priests there last night, but these guys were. As the jolly couple join us, I wonder if they'd be even jollier if last night's opening comedy set had been better.

'Hi!' says Matt with a handshake. It's the spectre from last night, but I make a conscious effort not to imply I've ever even met his mum.

The wee bookkeeper nudges Emily with her elbow, hitting slightly above her knee. 'He was one of those turns in your show.'

'Last night?' checks Emily. Here it comes. The accusation. How as a Christian can I utter such twisted words? Then the half-hour compulsory prayer session. 'Oh you weren't on first, were you? The babysitter kept us waiting – we only got there in the interval. I'm so sorry.'

I'm saved! A sentence often uttered in churches (though perhaps not often enough) – only here I'm saved from social embarrassment and quiet grumbly judgment.

'So you're a Christian?' Matt asks. 'Typical we missed it. How great that you can stand up there and be a positive influence. The other acts on the bill were all smut and being rude to hecklers.'

I stay silent. It's not the time or place to confess the truth (all right, I know it's exactly the time *and* the place).

Our conversation ends when Matt tells Emily to finish her coffee and fetch their coats. She obeys, which implies to me they were probably married in this church by today's minister.

So yes, I got away with it. Part of me feels cheated that the comeuppance I thought I'd get never came. For that brief moment, I knew I'd been caught out, until I wasn't. I'm sure in that audience of four hundred last night, there must have been one or two Christians there – I've just avoided meeting them. I know I deserve to be found out though, so I decide that one day, if I ever get to write a book about experiences of life on the road as a Christian comic, I should confess my reckless run-in with a heckler in those pages. One day ...

2

Local Hero

Uniting with the URC

I entered my third hour of being trapped in the unfamiliar bathroom.

The neighbourhood wasn't one I knew. If you'd have given me a hotline to the local police station, all I could've said was, 'I'm on the outskirts of Newcastle ... Well can you just try all the houses till you find me? I'm the one yelling through frosted glass with just a small travel towel for clothing. Yes, it *is* surprisingly compact for packing ... '

Life on the road necessitates staying with friends, especially when the gig fee barely covers the petrol. I normally try and bring a bottle of plonk as rent, but sometimes even the cost of that pushes the gig into becoming a loss maker.

Sofa-hopping means gatecrashing a lot of people's Saturday mornings, when no one gets much done. That was exactly what I was doing right now, and I'm sure I wasn't the only one in the street still not dressed at midday. Judging by the response to my hoarse shouts though, perhaps I was the only one in the street.

I generally try and travel light, but not this light. I had just a towel and a toilet bag; my clothes were a room and a world away. I had no help, no hope and no one in the house for two full days. Forty-eight hours! Two thousand eight hundred and eighty minutes![1]

Someone would miss me surely, and call for help. Well, no. I'd got a new girlfriend, Zoë, but when I said I was off to the north-east, she thought that meant Walthamstow. Besides, we were still at the stage where if I didn't call for five days, she'd just think I was playing 'hard to get'. In fact I was playing 'hard to get out'.

To be fair, I had been warned about this room. As soon as I'd arrived at Jo's on Friday afternoon, she'd said that the bathroom door was, 'a bit

---

[1] I had the gift of time, and sadly not the gift of a phone to calculate the seconds. Or call for help, which would have been more useful.

dodgy'. She'd reminded me too that she was leaving at dawn for a weekend away with friends, due to me mistiming my visit to the north-east. But I could come and go as I pleased till I left on Sunday morning. Fine in theory, but I couldn't come and go anywhere. She'd be back on Sunday night, which at the moment was looking like my best chance of escaping.

She'd explained very clearly that if I use the bathroom, don't, whatever I do, let the door completely shut. She was having some work done, the inside handle had been removed – and with it, all possibility of leaving, should the door close completely.

'Not a problem,' I'd said, and indeed early on Friday evening it was not a problem – my memory lasted the few minutes needed to apply this information.[2] Then came the gig: a pleasant arts centre show with two other acts. Except they were stuck in traffic and never arrived, so my twenty minute slot turned into an hour. The audience would never know the difference, until they looked at the poster on the way out and wondered where their twelve pounds had gone.[3]

So I'd dredged up old material and tried to remember new. I'd bantered with most of the audience, and after my poor brain had tried to hold a dozen or so audience names, as well as jokes from notebooks and from yesteryear, it's no wonder that when I arrived back, memory of the cursed bathroom door was all but gone.

Only tiredness meant I didn't slam it shut late that night, and I then took to my sofabed and curled up with a Choose Your Own Adventure book I'd plucked from Jo's bookcase.[4]

Saturday morning was not so kind. Jo had left early for her weekend trip, which I'm sure was genuine, and not just booked at the last minute because I'd announced I was turning up. Bleary-eyed, I'd staggered to the bathroom with a wash bag, a towel, a yawn, and the clothes I was born in. I pushed the door behind me ...

... and slam.

Ah.

My first thoughts were of disbelief: No, it must open – 'You'll get

---

[2] You may remember my bad memory from chapter one. If you've forgotten already, congratulations: your memory is as bad as mine.

[3] It hadn't gone to me, though the kind promoter tipped me an extra thirty quid for doing three times as long as originally booked for.

[4] Let this be a lesson – always take a book to the bathroom.

locked in' is just the sort of thing people *say*, it doesn't actually *happen*. Then panic: If I pull hard enough, it's bound to open through sheer desperation. Then a period of alternating prayer words and swear words.

I checked and double-checked the door, and Jo was right – once that latch had clicked into place, there was no budging it. The door was flush. Where once was a handle, there was now a hole about a centimetre in diameter, revealing a square gap that the mechanism of a door handle would fit into perfectly, had I one to hand.

Instead I had nothing, but time. With her gone for two days, I weighed my options:

- Shout. A neighbour would hear eventually. Maybe one that works as a 24-hour locksmith.
- Bash the door down. Granted, the only sizeable object in the room was a wicker laundry basket, but I reckoned that after several hours of insanity, I could do some serious damage with it.
- Dig. If it worked in *The Great Escape*, it could work here. I just needed a spade, a forged passport and a grasp of basic Geordie in case I was caught.[5]
- Make my peace with it. I wouldn't die here. In fact I'd probably picked the best room to be shut in – I had a working toilet, taps full of drinkable water, a bath to sleep in and toys to alleviate boredom. Jo's rubber ducky may have been bought ironically, but I figured I'd have quite a few chats with him over the next thirty-six hours. I even had toothpaste in my wash bag should I need some sustenance. I counted my blessings that I'd only just invested in a new tube of Aquafresh – enough for breakfast, lunch and a light hors d'oeuvres, and with the tri-stripe effect, I could pretend it was Neapolitan ice cream.

Well what would you do? I'll lay it out for you. You've got a handleless door. On the back of it is a hook. On the other side is freedom. To the right of the door is the sink, on which is a flannel, a beaker with a toothbrush, some toothpaste[6] and some squirty hand soap.

---

[5] Madness was already kicking in.
[6] More toothpaste! I shall dine well tonight …

Next along from the sink is the toilet. Nothing to see there. All right, there's the standard ballcock flush mechanism, but I can't see how that can be manipulated to make a working handle or crowbar, given no tools or DIY ability. Below there's a toilet brush and above is the bathroom cabinet. There's a frosted window, then the bath, with shower attachment over it and shower curtain across the side of it. At the foot end of the bath is the aforementioned wicker laundry basket, which brings us back to the door again. The evil door.

So how would you get out? Well, what played in my head was the book I was reading the night before: the Choose Your Own Adventure book. If you're new to the genre, it's quite self-explanatory. You, the reader, are on a quest and via various permutations and combinations you devise your own route. Traditionally the adventures would involve fighting goblins in a maze, or breaking out of a towering citadel. Here the adventure is far greater: only a few choices stand between you, and Escape From the Bathroom of Doom. This is no ancient castle; this is Newcastle.

Each quest used to last a whole book. This one's shorter, because there aren't many things in a bathroom. So, given the above room layout, and your inventory (a wash bag with duplicates of the above accessories, and a towel), what would you do first?

1

*If you opt for pulling the door very hard from the hook on the back of it, go to **2**.*

*If you choose to climb out of the window and lower yourself down with the shower curtain, go to **3**.*

*If you want to charge at the bathroom door with a heavy lump of porcelain, go to **6**.*

2

Well done, you've just broken the hook off the back of the door. Now you're stuck in a bathroom *and* you owe the owner a new hook. This is fast becoming the worst day this week. So what now?

*If you decide to have a go getting out of that window, go to **3**.*

*If you wish to investigate the sink area, go to **6**.*

3

You yank down the shower curtain from the bath. It's quite dramatic.

But just think for a moment. You've got no clothes on. When up against the window, that frosted glass doesn't protect the outside world from much, let alone if you're clambering out of it. What if some neighbour decides not to help, but to snap the event on their camera phone? Either way it's a moot point. The window's far too small to fit through. You really should have checked that before ripping down that shower curtain.

You wave the shower curtain out of the window for a little while, shouting as you do it, but stop after five minutes when you realise people must think you're beating a carpet while wailing to Motorhead.

If you want to wear some clothes from the laundry basket, go to **5**.

If you wish to pull the sink off the wall and throw it at the door, go to **6**.

4

Oh no! You're trapped in a time loop from another Choose Your Adventure Game. As the dark maze walls surround you, the riddling goblin in the distance gives a wild cackle. You tighten your clutch on the broadsword from the dragon's lair. To attempt escape from this temporal glitch, you have two choices:

Run left through the black hole, and hope to escape this broken record of time. Go to **4**.

Sidestep right into the wizard's force field, and utter the magic words: 'Will this eternal time-loop ever end?!' Go to **4**.

5

The laundry basket – home to clothes! They're not yours and they'll have been worn, but hey, it's getting nippy with that window open for three hours. You could close it, but look what happened last time you closed a thing. Door wouldn't open again. You approach the laundry basket thinking it may not help you escape, but it might keep you toasty and dignified as you plot your exit. Granted, Jo is female, and you're not,[7] but there are different levels of dignity. Dressing up in a woman's unwashed clothing is still a notch above where you currently are.

It's empty. Probably for the best.

If you want to know how you'd look if the laundry basket wasn't empty, go to **7**.

[7] Well, I'm not.

22

If you wish to assert your masculinity by trying to break the door down with the sink, go to 6.

6

You approach the sink. It's a sturdy unit, so sadly will not budge from the wall. Probably for the best – you'd have to explain why you've destroyed the bathroom, and you're not a home wrecker (I hope). The items on the sink just rattle a little as you shake. These wash-time accessories are more mobile, but less of a threat to the door. You can't charge at the door with a flannel. You can, but you'd look foolish.

Do you want to try charging at the door with a flannel? Go to 7.

Do you want to give that a miss and examine the toothbrush? Go to 8.

7

You look foolish. *Go to 8.*

8

The toothbrush on the sink belongs to Jo. You've got a similar one in your wash bag. They're not that different, although Jo's is clearly an upmarket version. It probably reaches teeth other brushes can't reach.[8] Your own toothbrush is in the wash bag, currently perched on the laundry basket, and is a budget version: splayed bristles, cheap plastic handle, not very comfy to hold as it's a long cuboid with rounded edges.

Hang on a sec. A long cuboid is just the mechanism needed to fit in that gap where the door handle once was. The spindle that would stretch from handle to handle would have been a cuboid too, and something of that shape and size *could* turn the latch.

Do you want to try the toothbrush as the spindle for the door latch? Go to 10.

Do you want to not bother trying it? Go to 9.

9

I really think you should try using the toothbrush as a spindle. *Go to 10.*

10

Full of hope, you try the toothbrush from the wash bag in the small hole where the door handle once was. Frustratingly, it doesn't quite fit. So

[8] It makes you wonder why they market other toothbrushes. 'Reaches 80% of all teeth' just doesn't cut it.

close, yet so far away. You try for several minutes, yelling, 'It must! It must fit! This has to be the way out!'[9]

Eventually, forlorn, you replace the too-large toothbrush and look elsewhere.

If you think it's a good idea to take the toilet ballcock apart, go to 11.
If you want to look in the cabinet above the WC, go to 13.

11

You dismantle the ballcock from the toilet cistern until it's in fifteen different pieces, and you have wet, yucky hands. What now, genius? This shtick might work for Jack Bauer, but you're just a bloke who can't even wire a plug. How are you going to turn this into a working door handle? What's more, you now owe Jo a new ballcock. 'You won't notice I'm here,' you said ...

Oh, and if you're stuck here for two days – which you deserve to be with this attitude – how are you going to flush that loo? New plan please.

To look in the bathroom cabinet, either for a spare ballcock or a means of escape, go to 13.

To practise sword fighting with the toilet brush, go to 12.

12

You take the toilet brush out of its vase, and start some mean fencing moves. It's woefully unhygienic, not very dignified and in no way helps your mission to leave this Stalag Luft of bathrooms. So unfortunately:

GAME OVER. You have lost the plot. Sorry. You can just keep reading though to see what other, better players would have done.

13

You (or I) wouldn't normally peek into someone else's bathroom cabinet, would you? But drastic times call for drastic measures. Inside you find an array of shampoos, a razor and razorblades, and a pack of cotton buds. If nothing else, when you finally leave the bathroom, you can be clean-shaven with silky smooth hair. You can't 'Wash & Go', but you can 'Wash'.

To investigate the razor further, go to 14.
To give up and sleep in the bath, go to 17.

---

[9] Bear in mind I actually did this.

14

You take the razor out of the cabinet. It probably won't help slice your way out of that door, like a painstakingly slow version of Jack Nicholson in *The Shining*: 'Heeeere's Johnny ... eventually.'

What the razor will do, though, is slice something smaller, like perhaps a toothbrush ...

To whittle the toothbrush with the razor until it fits the spindle hole in the door, go to **16**.

To use the toothbrush to brush the razor, go to **15**.

15

Now you have a clean razor. Pointless, but filled some time. *Go to* **16**.

16

You take the razor and start slicing the cuboid end of the toothbrush to make it fit that gap in the door. Thin slivers of plastic fall into the sink. You frequently try it in the spindle hole; if you take too much off, the toothbrush will rattle around in the cube gap, with no chance of ever turning that latch.

After a good five minutes of whittling, the toothbrush is taking shape. You try it in the door and ... it fits! One gentle turn of the brush, and it becomes an improvised door handle. The latch (praise be!) retracts into the door, and now you just need to pull the door open.

If you didn't tear the hook off the back of the door in option **2** *above, then the door opens and you may now leave. Success!*

If you did visit option **2** *above and tore it off, sorry, you're stuck here. Go to* **17**.

17

You make your peace with being prisoner here, climb into the bath, and pull the shower curtain up to your chin. Night, night (except it's day). *GAME OVER.*

* * *

Simple as that. For me, that took three and a half hours. And I felt good. I was a hero! I was MacGyver! I had found myself in a fix and combined the objects at my disposal to ensure my escape. Give me my man badge now.

When I'd danced for joy in every room I could, I wedged that bathroom door well and truly open with the wicker laundry basket. If I had to come back in here, there was no way I was being caught out again. Then again, even if I was, so long as my trusty whittled toothbrush was with me, I could come and go as I pleased. Maybe this is how cat burglars start.

Next was to eat some real food,[10] then seize my trusty phone. How I'd missed it – all those communication possibilities I took for granted. I felt like dialling everyone in my phone book, partly because I finally could and partly because I wanted to shout from the rooftop about how I'd found my freedom with just a razor and a toothbrush.

Instead I limited my phone calls to girlfriend Zoë, my dad, and finally the householder Jo. Zoë and dad were both happy to hear my tale, although didn't quite share my level of enthusiasm. Zoë humoured me but had to dash as she had lunch on the boil, so I think we left the story with her thinking I was still trapped in a bathroom in Walthamstow. My dad heard it all, but brought me back down to earth with the challenge that I may be able to escape a bathroom, but did I know how to change a tyre? I bet he has a man badge.

I left a voicemail for Jo, explaining briefly what had occurred. It was when I was preparing to go onstage at Saturday's gig – the same venue as Friday but now with three acts – that Jo texted back: 'Sorry to hear! Glad you made it out. You could have also looked behind the bath where I keep the spare handle.'

Oh, now that hurt.

I returned from the comedy night – a mixed performance from me, overjoyed at my new-found freedom, frustrated at the notion of this spare handle – and stormed immediately to the bathroom. Wicker basket still propping the door, and shaved toothbrush still in wash bag in case of a sudden draught and a slam, I checked behind the bath. It was a free-standing tub and there, nestled behind the pipes on the floor, a brass handle complete with spindle stared up at me.

I did a little cry. Hero status was no longer intact. Crying is something Jack Bauer and MacGyver rarely do, and they'd always, always, find the spare handle.

* * *

[10] It turns out toothpaste isn't that satisfying.

A day later, and I'm lost. Yesterday I couldn't find my way out of a bathroom; today I can't find my way into a church. I'm told there are at least three on this road, one of which is recommended by a friend of a friend.[11] It's apparently modern and funky and meets in a non-descript building on a non-descript road in a non-descript town. I've found the town at least and it's ... well I can't describe it. Let's stick with non-descript.

Apparently their meetings pack the village hall to the rafters. Unfortunately only locals know it because whenever they put a sign up saying 'church', it gets stolen. That's breaking at least a couple of the Ten Commandments: it's stealing, it doesn't exactly help others to 'remember the Sabbath day', and if they secretly covet the signs for themselves (unlikely), then that's bad too.

I've done more U turns than a cabinet minister. A shaved toothbrush won't help me here, and my satnav is shrugging. Where is this place? Clearly they're emulating those modern and funky nightclubs that no one knows how to find, and when you do it's just a door and a keypad.[12]

There's a general 10.30 a.m. deadline when finding churches. Some might start at 11 a.m., but there's no guarantee. It's nerve-wracking enough walking in alone to an unfamiliar church; it's worse to do it ten minutes late when they're giving a church news item about '... Outreach, so more strangers come into our building'. Cue me. Everyone looks and gasps.

It's 10:27. I've got my failsafe option of the local cinema showing a substandard rom-com at 11 a.m., but I'll just feel bad that I'm missing church to watch Matthew McConaughey 'hilariously' woo Kate Hudson.

I see a spire! That must be it. It's not very non-descript, so it could just be *a* church rather than *the* church, but a) beneath that rickety steeple might be the most funky modern spiritual youth this side of the non-descript town, and b) it's 10:28 and it really doesn't matter. I just want to get my praise on and avoid McConaughey.

[11] 'Four stars, a sermon not to miss.'
[12] I've once been to such a beyond-fashionable club, in New York. It was owned by a family friend – the only way I'd ever get on the guest list – and the taxi driver was convinced there was nothing on this street but bins. When we were dropped off, it was just door after door of nothing: no signs, no noise spilling into the street. The only clue was after five minutes when Brad Pitt pulled up in a car and rang a bell, so we followed him. It was a good night, eventually.

I'm particularly keen on some God chat this morning, partly to give thanks for (and, all right, brag about in prayer) my escape from the bathroom, and partly to ask why, in His infinite wisdom, He couldn't have arranged for Jo to leave the spare handle somewhere more obvious. I've asked Jo the same question and her answer – 'Well, *I* knew it was there,' – wasn't satisfying.

I navigate my way to the spire, which turns out to be atop an old, large, very traditional building. I park outside and jog up the grand steps to the door, where I follow in a suited pensioner.[13]

As I draw near, I read the sign above the door: 'United Reformed Church'. This could be the modern funkiness my friend's friend told me about. Perhaps the pensioner's about to start some body popping. It's unlikely, because from what I recall, the 'URC' has been around a while ...

Putting the 'URC' in 'CHURCH' (otherwise it's just 'CHH')

- *General ejection.* Oliver Cromwell stirred up some vicars, causing The Great Ejection. It's nothing to do with people in dog collars being flung from planes, which is a shame because that's an interesting image. It's actually about mainstream Anglicans being ousted from churches to make way for maverick ministers called Congregationalists and Presbyterians, which is nowhere near as funny as priests in ejector seats.

- *Presbyteriwho?* Presbyterians don't have the Church of England's bishops (or archbishops) or deacons (or archdeacons), but that doesn't make them enemies (or archenemies). Instead they have a 'presbytery': not, as it sounds, a church café, but an assembly of elected elders. Scotland is the home of the Presbyterians, who I think had a hit with 'I Would Walk 500 Miles'.

- *And Congregationaliwhatyousay?* Congregational churches go even further – and I don't mean 501 miles. I mean they're governed by the congregation, hence the name. Wales is the

---

[13] Unlike the trendy New York nightclub, the man I follow in isn't Brad Pitt, unless it's Brad Pitt in the early scenes of *The Curious Case of Benjamin Button*.

biggest Congregationalist area in Europe. They have lots of independent churches who don't talk to each other, probably in part because of all the mountains.

- *Let's be civil.* King Charles II hid in an oak tree (hence The Royal Oak pubs), and upon emerging victorious as Hide-and-Seek champion of 1651, he gave the Anglicans their churches back from the Cs and Ps, who became rebels without a church. In 1662 these rebels (about a fifth of clergy) were told to adopt the Book of Common Prayer and the Thirty-Nine Articles by St Bartholomew's Day (24 August, as I'm sure you know). They refused and set up on their own.
- *United as in Manchester, reformed as in ham.* Congregationalists and Presbyterians united in 1972 to form the United Reformed Church. There's not a head of the URC as such, but there is a moderator. At the time of writing it's Val Morrison, who on a regular basis can be heard to say, 'No, it's Val, and no I don't know any Brown-Eyed Girl.'

The gatekeepers[14] are both in their sixties yet still among the youngest here. Despite the large interior being fairly empty, it's a warm and cosy atmosphere. It feels like we're one Werther's Original away from a grandparent convention. I consider leaving my coat on, then take it off, knowing that my fellow congregants would be the first to suggest that I wouldn't feel the benefit. Glancing at some of the congregants, I optimistically think, 'Yeah, these guys could be the modern funky kind.'

I take a pew near the back – it is literally one person per pew. I begin to wonder if the service starts at 11 a.m., which might explain the lack of people ... and then the minister begins.

'How lovely it is to see some new faces!' he declares, while looking directly at me. He means 'new face'. There's an audible shuffle as many in the congregation turn to look, and I give an embarrassed nod to the dozen OAPs.

I'm grateful when the organ strikes up with some worship greatest hits, and happily they're all *Songs of Praise* classics I'm familiar with. You don't want to be a newbie mumbler. I'm starting to think, though, that

---

[14] I've read too many Choose Your Own Adventure Books.

maybe this isn't the funky church I was recommended, unless 'Crown Him with Many Crowns' is about to get a serious remix.

Reading, sermon and prayers are all traditional and short to make way for communion, which with this number here will be pretty brief too. The sign of peace is trickily executed. We're meant to shake hands with our nearest neighbours, but due to age and low attendance, everyone's spread out and mostly immobile. I do more moving than most and manage seven 'Peace be with you's, feeling bad for the four I've left out. I throw a smile at each of them as if to say, 'Catch you later.' I nearly add a wink, but thankfully stop myself.

Things begin to differ from what I'm used to. I don't think it's just a URC thing, 'cos we're mavericks', but rather than queue up at the altar for our bread and wine, we stay seated and it comes to us. The demographic may mean it makes sense to do the meals-on-wheels version of the Lord's Supper, rather than uprooting everyone. The paraphernalia, though, implies this is more greatly ingrained, since the sidesmen are passing around racks of wine-filled glasses. They resemble the test tube racks we used to have at school, only specially crafted to hold a number of miniature shot glasses.

It sounds flippant to describe it as such: the truth is that I hold communion very dear as a great practical means of fellowship with God, and with our fellow man. It always bonds me with those I'm communing with, and I now realise that it's not the queuing up that causes that bond, nor is it receiving it from a chalice at the altar, much as this forms one of the few arcane rituals that I actually embrace taking part in. It must be some other aspect of this Holy Eucharist that stirs my soul, because as I take my individual shot of wine from the rack, with a small morsel of bread from a plate that follows it, this still feels every bit as special.

The rack and plate passes to the next row and for the first time I find myself with communion bread and wine in my own hands, rather than proffered by servers at the altar. I am thankful for this community's welcome as one of their own, and take in the bread and wine in prayer. I consume and commune with God.

I remain in prayer for some minutes, giving over to the Almighty the events of the weekend – my safe journey across the country, my confinement and freedom, and my opportunity to tell jokes to some Geordies. The near-empty church makes my moment of personal prayer as distraction-free as any time I can remember.

My prayer time is only brought to an end by the minister's words:

'Now we take the bread in our hands and say together, "This is the body of Christ, the bread of heaven".'

All join in with a mumble on those last words. All apart from me: I stay slack-jawed and silent. I have no bread in my hands. I've eaten it.

I think I've found something this church does differently.

I look around, and see everyone taking and eating. A couple look towards me and notice I'm not. I go as crimson as the wine that everyone else is holding.

The congregation continue: 'This is the blood of Christ, the cup of salvation.'

I don't know if it's right for me to join in saying this – I've already said my own version, to myself and to God, a few minutes ago. Should I say it again, in unison? But I want to join in with the others – communion is communal after all. I quickly decide to murmur something similar, changing it to past tense: 'This was the blood of Christ ...'

I panic that I've committed a heresy. It's eternal surely? Just because I've consumed it, that doesn't change anything. I need to speak to a bishop. And I'm in a URC – they don't believe in bishops. Let me speak to the moderator. Does anyone have Val Morrison's phone number? It must be 0800 SHA-LA-LA-LA-LA-LA-LA-LA-LA-LA-LA-TE-DA ...

I add: 'And still is.'

As they drink, I'm now miming, pretending I have a full glass. It sounds awful, but I want to save face. I can't be the newcomer who barges in and guzzles bread and wine like some kind of hungry interloper. It surely comes off that I'm just here for the free food and drink. That looks terrible (although I'm sure that as good Christians they'd welcome and feed me).

Part of me is very glad that's over. I was having a great communion till everyone else joined in.

The service ends with some notices, and my word there's a lot going on. Looking around, I can't see that many of the senior citizens are interested in toddler dance, step aerobics or the drop-in breastfeeding clinic, although one elderly lady went, 'Ooh!' at the sound of Zumba. There's a more audible response to the Tuesday lunch club and Thursday's seafront saunter.

We're dismissed and a dear lady in Sunday best introduces herself as Janet. Worried she'll mention my Eucharistic faux pas, I quickly ask about her life here. She retired locally fifteen years ago, and is fiercely proud of their events. Far from being a stranger to toddler dance and the breastfeeding clinic, Janet is a regular – she provides the tea. Zumba and step aerobics don't get tea. They probably bring their own organic watercress juice.

Janet is proud of the other groups they host, an impressive list: antenatal classes, playgroup, Brownies, Scouts, ballet, Alcoholics Anonymous, Narcotics Anonymous … It sounds like the *Seven Ages of Man*, directed by Ken Loach.

'There's plenty here for you,' Janet encourages with a twinkle in her eyes.

'Oh no,' I hasten to add. 'I'm not local.'

She's not put off. 'Oh, well come back anyway. We need young men. And we're starting Bhangra soon.'

A jovial gentleman joins her, a junior at this church at about sixty. 'I've come to meet the new recruit!'

'I'm just passing through,' I say with a smile, before adding, 'but thanks for having me.' The generation gap means I feel like I'm over playing at a friend's house, and the illusion is completed when Janet hands me a piece of cake on a paper plate.

As I thank her, she turns to Mr Jovial. 'We were saying he's going to come back.'

'Was I?' I quickly add through a mouthful of lemon drizzle.

'Good!' says Mr Jovial. 'Has he met Alice?'

'Ooh no, I must get her!'

Janet scurries off to a huddle of people near the front. I edge doorwards, but Mr Jovial is slightly blocking my exit.

'You'll like Alice. She's about your age.'

I see where this is going, so try and change the subject. 'Lovely service. I must come back here *with my wife* if we're up this way.' I don't have a wife but I do have a girlfriend, who's great and doesn't live four hundred miles away. I could have mentioned her rather than a 'wife', but I panicked – a shame as it's bound to be a sin to fib in church, but after my earlier heresy, all bets are off.

'Yes, you should bring your wife,' says Mr Jovial with a squint, or it could be a wink. 'Only you haven't met her yet.'

That didn't work then. I like to think the lack of wedding ring gave me away, but I fear it's the *Red Dwarf* T-shirt and smell of Lynx. Janet's now back in view, dragging by the arm a woman who's clearly reluctant, fifteen years my senior, and Alice. Janet didn't mention speed dating among their church activities.

'Well, it's been lovely to come and visit,' I say to Mr Jovial, finishing my cake and edging doorwards. 'Thanks.'

Janet sees me making a beeline and is really yanking at Alice's arm now. She's not quick enough though. Despite Janet's stealth moves and Mr Jovial's last-ditch attempt to block the door, I'm out and down those steps quicker than you can say 'whittled toothbrush'.

Looking at the church from the safety of my car, I notice again its vast size. Such a big building for a congregation of barely the number of disciples, for today at least. Yet my friend of a friend told me of at least three local churches who are building-less. They meet in disused halls, pub function suites or university lecture rooms. Should this dwindling church 'give up' their considerable space, so that the overflowing congregations down the road can have a place of their own? I don't know even if the younger, funkier gatherings would want a building like this – I love the traditional architecture of it and the fact that the spire is a beacon in the community (it called *me* in), but does everyone?

I think the answer is in what Janet told me a few minutes ago. Her list of groups who use the church was strikingly all-encompassing. You may rattle around in this building on a Sunday morning, but come back tomorrow and you'll find toddlers making way for dance classes, and dance classes making way for Narcotics Anonymous. Maybe, if you're lucky, Narcotics Anonymous might join in with Zumba and we'd all feel part of something amazing.

First impressions can be deceptive. Is this a thriving or dying church? Or is it missing the point to judge it by its Sunday service? I've heard Christians talk about the 'broken world', as if it's distant. It's not – it's on our doorstep. The AA, the playgroup, the antenatal classes – they're in a sanctuary within these walls. The sheer number of events for the non-churched in this venue shows that church in a community does work. What other building can offer so much?

As if to answer my question, I head to the local pub for a roast dinner and a read of the papers.

I enter and expect glares and for the piano to stop playing, but I feel surprisingly at home here now. Having spent a good deal of time in the north-east – most of it trapped in a toilet – I feel like one of the locals. Not too much though: it's only a few degrees outside, so they're all in vests, while I reach for my coat …

My coat. I took it off to feel the benefit, and it's still in the pew. It's Sunday afternoon and I expect the church to be locked, but I'm not here often and the coat is by a fancy designer called George. The locals may not even have seen a coat before – it could be in a museum by now.

The church door is unlocked when I reach it, so I tentatively push it open. It looks like no one's in.

'Ssh.'

It's Alice, the woman that Janet, Mr Jovial and the great URC prophecy of 1740 had hoped would pair off with me.[15] She gestures through the entrance lobby into the main church, where I now see three adults and a child.

'Access visit,' she whispers to me.

I nod and ask quietly about my coat. As Alice becomes a garment-fetching ninja, I glance at the family and see who this church is really here for. Its people aren't just those on a Sunday who take communion together (or on their own); there are also others who need it, whether to learn Indian dancing or to spend time with their child following a separation. They need neutral ground, and what better ground than this?

Alice returns with my coat. I thank her and judge that, despite Janet's matchmaking, she's not that keen anyway. I don't think she likes *Red Dwarf* or Lynx, which is just as well.

I'm about to head for home, then think I'd better use the facilities before crossing the country.

Down the corridor and up the stairs, I find the Gents and lock the door. Yesterday's handle incident jolts back to me, and I decide to unlock the door quickly just to check.

It doesn't budge.

'Alice!!!!!!'

[15] If you remember the earlier information box, you may be thinking there was no URC in 1740. Five points to you.

3

The Show Must
Mynd Ymlaen

Worshipping with the Welsh

I broke for the border, pursued by police cars.

Then the police cars overtook me and I trundled on to the Severn Bridge tollbooth. The long drives get boring, so you have to add a bit of glamour where you can. Thankfully I was soon to be picking up a couple of comics to help while away the rest of the journey to far-west Wales, but first I had the bridge's troll to pass.

'Afternoon,' I offered from my billy goat's car. The troll – a bearded hulk of a man with bags for life under his eyes – didn't reply, and just carried on chewing. He held out a sugary hand, with no need to say anything to the umpteenth customer in a row, thanks to the fixed price.

I handed over coin after coin for admission to the giant theme park of Welshland, wondering what I'd get for my cash. Maybe a smile? No. What about a receipt?

My question made him swallow his pastille whole, so he could reply for the first time in hours. 'We don't give receipts. Oh, and we don't accept two pence pieces either.'

I'd only handed over five of them, but it seemed they'd ceased to be legal tender. 'Oh. Well, I haven't got anything else.'

'Haven't you got 10p?'

'Yes,' I replied. 'In 2ps. Aren't they real money?'

'Well, barely,' came the terse reply as he reached for another sweet.

I looked at the coppers in my hand, confused. They looked like real coins.

'Do you take cards?' I asked.

'No,' he said, chewing on the next one. 'Come on, you must have a ten pence piece.'

I wanted to do a dozen things. I wanted to stare his beardy face down till he cracked and let me into Wales for ten pence cheaper. I wanted to see if he'd call his boss to okay a two pence-based transaction. I wanted to mutter something about him being racist for not taking brown coins.

Unfortunately, his eyesight was better than mine.

'What's that in your change drawer? By the sweet wrappers?'

He may have looked weary but he was sharp as a lemon pastille. A dirty ten pence piece stared up at me. With a heavy heart I handed it over and the barrier lifted.

Next time I'd plan ahead my monetary stand-off. It may be petty but this, like all good protests, was about change.

I stopped in Cardiff to pick up two of the other three comics for that night's show. I was both compère and designated driver for two Welsh acts: musical comic Katie, who was opening, and lanky student Dennis who was travelling for five minutes of stage time and no money. Andy, the headliner, was driving from Birmingham, or so we thought till Katie received a text from him.

'What's the gig postcode?' Katie asked from the passenger seat.

'Er, SA61 something,' I replied, pulling away into Cardiff traffic. 'Why?'

'Andy put the wrong postcode in his satnav. He's halfway to S61.'

'Where's that then?' asked Dennis from the back.

I tried it on my satnav. 'Rotherham,' I reported.

Both postcodes were coincidentally for 'High Street', so it was an easy enough mistake to make, but one that had sent Andy several hours north-east from his Midlands home, rather than south-west to where we were.

We headed west on the motorway into the setting sun, and chuckled impishly at Andy's misfortune. Because that's what comedians in cars do.

Comedy car-shares: a bluffer's guide
Great for sharing petrol costs and gig stories, most comedy car-shares go roughly the same way …

1. 'Been busy?' (i.e. Are you playing the same gigs as I am?)
    Always be humble about how you did at these gigs – no one likes a boaster. Your co-travellers would much rather hear you say:

'Tough gig, that.'

than:

'You know what, everyone else suffered, but they needed to call a tiler after my set cos I took the roof off.'

2. 'Been to this one before?' (i.e. Anticipation of the gig to come.)

Honesty counts here.

'Last time I was here we only had seven in. It was awful,' ... is fine.

As is ... 'This guy never pays on time.'

3. 'Did you hear about ...?' (i.e. Tales of suffering.)

Expect to hear of unpopular comedians doing badly at gigs, of comics refusing to pay petrol money so being abandoned at petrol stations, and of just how much money each act lost at Edinburgh Festival last year. Most comedians' cars are powered by Schadenfreude alone.

4. 'You know what happened to me today...' (i.e. Suspiciously convenient 'true stories'.)

If any topic comes up that is not directly related to the comedy industry, there's every chance you'll hear the story/opinion/turn of phrase again later that evening as part of the comic's act. You'll recognise it and feel affronted, that what you thought was a light chat between you earlier, was actually a performer trying out some new material. Never trust a comedian with a pen in his hand.

Just shy of the coast, we reached our destination. We hadn't needed the satnav: directions like, 'Take the M4 west and don't drown,' would have sufficed. This was the Welsh Land's End. This was Lland's End.

I fed the parking meter, even after 6 p.m. and Katie and Dennis threw money in, which was helpful because it was yet another automaton that didn't accept two pence pieces.

'I hate paying to park,' sniffed Katie. 'The way they go on about carbon emissions, they should be paying us to stop the car.'

We strolled into the social club – a tired function room in need of a lick of paint and an audience – and the promoter bounded over with an outstretched hand. Comedians prefer the promoter's hand to have a stuffed envelope in it, but that would hopefully come later.

'So, this is it!' exclaimed promoter Darren, an excitable Londoner who seemed a long way from home.

Right, where's the audience, the three of us thought. He could tell, as our eyes scanned the empty seats.

'Don't worry, doors only opened twenty minutes ago. If we build it, they will come!'

Not necessarily. I've been at dozens of gigs where they didn't come, where the motto might have been better off as, 'If we advertise it, they've got a chance of showing up'. A lot of comics have an unwritten rule that ten's the magic number for audience numbers. Less than that and maybe it's best to cancel. A show with four in the audience is likely to be improved by us all just parting company and thinking of something funny for a couple of hours.

'What's your cut-off?' asked Katie. 'Less than ten and we pull it?'

'Pull what?' babbled Darren. 'You're all a bit wild, after a 'pull' here! Seriously though ... what? We've never pulled the night.'

'Do you think we'll get more if we wait?' I asked. By 'more' I meant 'some'.

'Oh yes,' said Darren. 'Show must go on and all that!'

No, it mustn't. We'd all driven four-plus hours for this. A nine hour round trip. Yes, we'd like a show at the end of it, but a function room that can fit two hundred but actually houses anyone we can pull in off the streets does not a show make.

A non-comedy person[1] might wonder what made us all take this gig, presuming it must be particularly well-paid, or a favour for a mate. Nope. This is normal. Only normally at least one person shows up.

Katie took charge. 'Darren, I think maybe we should pick a figure. If we get just an old man and his dog, best not do the show, yeah?'

Darren's jolly grin melted into a bouncer's glare, which he fixed on me. 'You want to get paid, you do the show.' The grin returned. 'You can cancel, but you all go home empty-handed. I've got a living to make.'

So did we, but we also had dignity to keep. I was sure the hypothetical old man and his dog wouldn't contribute enough to pay all our wages.

---

[1] Or 'muggle', as we often call them.

'Trust me, this happens every month. Friday night round here, they're all in the pub next door.' Darren spoke as if this was meant to reassure us. 'When the show starts, they all start coming in then. You get it started, they'll hear you through the wall and come running like Pavlov's dogs or whatever.'

I realised he was looking straight at me; I'd forgotten that I was compère. It would be my job to be Pied Piper and lure in next door's supposed revellers.

'I don't think that's a good idea,' I protested. 'I've done gigs to two people. I think I've done one to one. But I'm not going on to literally no one.'

Darren produced some envelopes from his donkey jacket. 'I've got your money here. For the end of the show.' He replaced it in his pocket and looked at us knowingly.

This was awful. In years on the comedy circuit, I'd never known of a promoter on such a completely different page as the comedians. He was in a different book. Ours was *The Complete Guide to Saving Face* and his was *Getting a Bad Name for Yourself: A Bluffer's Guide*.

'I'll start marshalling them,' Darren said, exiting into the street. And then there were three.

'Are a lot of gigs like this?' asked newbie Dennis.

'No,' Katie and I answered in unison.

We discussed, dissected and thought up some interesting names for promoter Darren, as well as questioning if any channels were making prank shows and where they were hiding the cameras if so. We concluded that, after coming this far, we wanted our cash. Dennis wasn't being paid, but for some reason he still wanted the stage time, even though it could potentially be to zero people. He could do that at home.

'So we're doing it,' concluded Katie. 'In which case, shall we get a move on? We could wait for the audience, but I think they're waiting for us ...'

'Darren!' I called, marching to the door. Let's get this so-called gig over with.

I left the venue and glanced into the pub next door. Sure enough, a handful of people were there: maybe twenty or so. Enough for a show, certainly, if all came through. Darren was being ignored by one table of girls, leaving a flyer on their table.

'Darren, shall we start?'

'Great, cheers Paul. I've flyered everyone. Now let's see you do your magic. Oh, and plug the disco.'

'The what?'

'The disco.' He handed me a flyer. Sure enough, this was being marketed as 'Comedy & Disco with DJ Darren'.

'I don't know that there'll be enough of them for a disco, even if all this lot bring a friend.'

'Got to have the disco, Paul. It's on the flyer. There's no "lie" in "flyers". Apart from the middle bit.' Darren looked at the flyer. 'Actually the middle bit is a lie – the open spot changed to this Dennis fella when Sarah Walson cancelled. Probably for the best – our crowd are discerning. Two women on the same bill – that wouldn't work.'

Darren was giving me more to loathe about him by the second. I instantly envied Sarah Walson and her cancellation.

Returning next door, I showed Katie and Dennis the flyer. 'Have you seen this?'

'Yeah,' Katie said. 'That's why no one's turned up. Flyer's not in Welsh.'

'Good evening, good evening! Ladies and gentlemen, boys and girls, oh no that's right, there's no one here. My name's Paul Kerensa, what are your names? What's that – I can't hear you … Oh no that's right, there's no one here. Well it's nice to be here. Is it? You lot have got the right idea, you're somewhere else. As you can tell, I've been touring lately with The Proclaimers. You wouldn't get that because a) You're not in this room so can't see that I look like one of The Proclaimers, and b) There is no 'you'. I don't know if you can hear this next door, but WE'VE STARTED!! Finish your drinks, show time has begun, currently there is a ginger Cornishman ripping this room apart – not in the metaphorical audience-rousing way, but literally ripping it apart as I vent my frustration on the function room furniture. And good evening comedians. Good of you to hide backstage, so that I am literally performing to nobody. Yeah, laugh it up. I'm just glad someone's laughing. Even the promoter has sodded off next door to drag the unsuspecting punters through. I was promised they'd come in if I started talking. Two minutes now. This is comedy gold you're missing here, next door, you hear?! All right, comedy bronze. So let's try some banter. What do you do for a living? Oh no that's right, THERE'S NO ONE HERE!'

The front door opened. Crowds of people could have suddenly poured in, but it was the promoter Darren.

'You haven't mentioned the disco.'

... and he vanished again.

'So have we got a show for you, yes and you know what else? Only the most exclusive disco in town! DJ Darren will be spinning the discs – don't know if he does requests, he doesn't want to get swamped, so don't all rush at once. Yes indeed, as soon as the show's over, it's party time – I know I'll be in a party mood, back on the M4. So, how long do you think I can keep this up?!'

Ten minutes was the answer. Ten long minutes of me talking to wallpaper, and bad wallpaper at that. Even the moose head frowned back at me. The acts waiting in the storage room alternately sniggered and wondered what they'd do if and when I eventually brought them on. But ten minutes in, as promised, the audience trickled in. Eight people in all – still under the threshold of ten that makes a comedy audience quorate.

The promoter rejoined us a few minutes after the eighth and final audient sat down. He was sweating, like he'd literally hunted this lot down from Lland's End town centre. He threw me a shrugged look: this was it. Three groups: five girls out for a good night; two lads who seemed to be following the girls; and the mandatory old man, this time without a dog.

I introduced Katie and her guitar, and relaxed a little. The nightmare gig was someone else's problem for twenty minutes – or more likely seventeen, tops.

'Nice gig?' asked Dennis the open spot, joining us in the main room finally.

'Have you done many gigs?' I asked back.

'About eight. Well, eight.'

'Yeah, all gigs aren't like this. This is weird.'

'... Don't you hate paying to park?' Katie said to the 'crowd'. She was nearing the end of her set. 'The way they go on about carbon emissions, they should be paying us to stop the car!'

Nothing from the punters – just an irked sound from me as I realised she'd used us earlier to try out new material.

'Well you've been ... an audience. Nearly. Goodnight!'

Katie leapt offstage and I brought Dennis straight on. We'd both

41

decided it best to skip the interval and capitalise on the momentum that wasn't there.

Dennis blitzed through his eight-minute set in three minutes. It's a good job we didn't have a middle section – with just him and his three minutes, I'd have had to do a lot of filling.

Dennis joined Katie and me in the storage room, his eyes wide and beaming.

'Great gig,' he said. 'Although I got through my set in record time. So much quicker when they're not laughing.'

Suits us, Katie and I thought – we can leave earlier.

Darren poked his head round the door. 'Andy's here.' And he vanished again, presumably to barricade the door from any punters with itchy feet.

I turned to Katie and Dennis. 'Andy. We should have probably let him know the gig wasn't worth the drive.'

'What do you mean?' said Dennis. 'It's rocking out there!'

Katie and I genuinely didn't know if he was being serious. Dennis was a little too enthusiastic to be joking.

'I should have texted him,' Katie conceded, and headliner Andy shambled in with heavy coat and bags.

'Birmingham to Rotherham to the Atlantic Ocean, for this,' he said morosely.

He looked back at the bare room and swore quietly. He then swore loudly when we told him that the audience weren't just small in number because of the interval – this was it. We kept the break short so as not to lose too many punters, and sure enough did lose two of the girls to the bar next door. I introduced Andy to an audience of six.

As he neared his big finish, which I've seen him storm to audiences of five hundred, the worst promoter in the world sidled up to me and whispered, 'Now I need you to pad for five minutes while I get the disco set up.'

Bless Darren's optimism. 'I don't think they're going to stay for the disco,' I said. 'The girls have been putting their coats on while Andy's on.'

'I promised them a disco on the flyer. I always deliver.'

That would be a good idea – he could be a delivery driver, because he was really good at making sure people stayed at home.

Andy left the stage saying, 'Please, no encore,' and one of the male punters eloped with one of the girls out of the venue. I took the stage to the dwindling applause of one old man, one young man, and two girls who still thought this was Lland's End's premier night out. Dennis's enthusiastic clapping helped too.

'Have you had a good night?' I asked in vain. An attempt at a cheer came back. 'Well your night's not over yet, because DJ Darren is preparing the finest disco tunes this side of the Welsh border. You like 'YMCA'? Well we've got enough for a letter each. I'll be the full stop. Is this thing on?'

It actually wasn't on, as Darren confirmed: 'Sorry, needed the feed for the disco mixer.'

'Cheers, Darren.'

I continued ad-libbing for far longer than a compère ever should at the end of the night, while Darren fumbled with cables and the punters began to fade back into the night. The old man finished his tankard and headed back next door. The remaining girls gossiped about which of the town's two nightclubs to go to, and the one man left tried to overhear. I waffled on throughout, like an audio screensaver. All three had their coats on, and I was mentally fetching mine too.

Darren, headphones around his neck, gave me the thumbs up.

Mid-joke, I cut to, ' ... Thank you and good night!' and ran offstage.

DJ Darren was heard through the speakers. 'Good evening, folks, got your favourite party tunes on a Friday night! First up, a classic from 1987!'

The door closed as the last guy followed the last girl out into the street. The comedians could be heard in the store room grumbling. The only ones left in the room were DJ Darren and me.

I could make up the song that played next. I could pretend for the sake of hindsight that Darren's disco started with something comedically convenient. But I have no need to rewrite history, because what I heard was the instantly recognisable percussion, bass and 'Woo!' of Whitney Houston's 'I Wanna Dance With Somebody'.

I looked at Darren, and he looked at me. Houston, we have a problem ... As the only two people left, we had a little dance. [2]

* * *

[2] All right, I made up the bit about the dance.

43

Twelve hours have passed since The Gig from Purgatory. It wasn't any worse than that, since it was just about tolerable, and no one needed to go to A&E. Someone might need to go to court over the Trade Descriptions Act due to calling it a comedy club.

I got paid – oh you'd better believe I got paid. I patiently waited for Whitney to finish, then grabbed my envelope and pegged it back to my car. The wodge sat in my back pocket and dug in on the drive east, but I was too tired to do anything about it. It was a good reminder of why we'd come here in any case.

Thanks to a combination of exhaustion, rain and Katie's suggestion of the finest curry South Wales could offer, I awake on Dennis's sofa, somewhere near Bridgend. I said I'd be up and gone early, and true enough Dennis hasn't roused before I'm gone.

Not far from his place, I find a delightful clifftop chapel, with nothing near it but a van selling delightful bacon sandwiches. The church seems out on its own, a fair hike to any village, with no apparent parish or target congregation. The location would make a great Bond chase, with a lone priest emerging from the church to shake his fist as cars hurtle around the Welsh coast, masquerading as Monaco.

The building bucks the trend of churches by facing west, since it would look rude to turn its back on the Bristol Channel. Most western churches face the other direction to greet the rising sun (from the east), and also to greet the rising Son (from Jerusalem). The theory goes that when Jesus returns, he'd come to Jerusalem – that's not biblical, I should point out, just 'common sense' along the lines of:

'I've decided to find Jesus.'

'Well where did you last see Him?'

'Erm, Jerusalem?'

Not only that, but graves traditionally face east too, so that when we're resurrected from the dead, we're facing the right way to get to Jerusalem to meet Jesus. Always good to have a headstart over some chump in the next cemetery who wakes up facing the wrong way.

They'd have a long way to walk from here – we seem far from anywhere. Yet a few folks do come, so I'm reassured a service is happening, I leave my car parked facing America, and enter the small chapel.

It resembles a Church of England building, which seems at odds given we're in Wales, but then I suppose we had a Bank of Scotland in

44

Guildford till recently. A sign tells me that this is the Welsh form of Anglicanism, the handily-named 'Church in Wales'. A further, more temporary sign, reads:

May-July & September
10.30 a.m. HC first Sun of month, except Aug-Sept 9.30 a.m.
or
10 a.m. MW at St Mary's 2nd/4th Suns
except when AA

It's then repeated in Welsh. Both make equal sense to me: I think it means they might be open today.

They are – it's full. It only holds thirty or so people, but these pews are overflowing. I perch at the back, until a woman sees and moves her dog so I can sit down. I quickly check the room again, and see that everyone else here is indeed human, as I take my seat.

The minister walks down the short aisle. He smiles at each of us and doesn't seem to recognise me as new, or any others as regular. He reaches the front, checks his watch and begins speaking. In Welsh.

Time passes. I await an English translation, like on airlines. After five minutes of solid Welsh – and this could be just the Welsh word for 'welcome' as far as I know – I fear that if there is a translation afterwards, this could be the longest service I've ever been to.

No translation comes, as everyone stands for the first hymn. I anticipate 'Guide Me O Thou Great Redeemer', hoping a male voice choir will pop up out of nowhere to sing, 'Feed me till I want no more!', but instead it's an unfamiliar hymn that sounds a good few centuries old. I couldn't catch the hymn number, so I flounder through the book for most of the song. I think it's in English, although it might be Welsh or even Aramaic.

We kneel for prayers, and the dog sits. My guess is that the other congregants understand Welsh, as they're a good second or two ahead of me on everything. Even the dog seems more clued up. It reminds me that it's only since 'Vatican II'[3] in the 1960s that Catholic services have been in local languages. Before that, unless you knew your Latin, good luck to you.

---

[3] Aka the Second Vatican Council. 'Vatican II' is not like *Thunderbird 2* or *Apollo 11*, although I suspect the Pope is hiding some kind of craft in St Peter's Basilica.

The minister changes his tone, and although I don't understand the words, I realise I should sit up and open my eyes. The sound of the other pews creaking is a big clue. More Welsh is spoken, and just as I think that I'm starting to understand Welsh for the first time, I realise the minister is translating into English for me. He must have seen the glazed look in my eye and deduced that it was different from the normal glazed look some have in church.

'We're going to have the choir sing a hymn now,' the vicar says, addressing me directly.

Two-thirds of the congregation stand and move to the front. They're the choir. I glance at those left: it's like we're parents and our Von Trapp children are putting on a show for us.

It's a pleasant Welsh song, a perfect accompaniment for the view outside the chapel. Close your eyes and you could be in a field far away from anywhere, largely because we are.

The choir rejoin us and the reading is announced, again in local dialect. Everyone opens their Bibles with a rustle, and the vicar leans towards me and says: 'Matthew 18.'

I open a thankfully English Bible in the chair pocket in front of me and turn to the relevant page. The Parable of the Lost Sheep. Well it would be, in rural Wales. They probably have this every week.

There follows ten minutes of Welsh, which I presume is the sermon, during which I'm guessing the vicar unpacks the passage we have or haven't heard, judging by how he gestures back to his open Bible. As he closes, he turns to me as if he's just remembered I'm there.

'Oh,' he says. 'I was just saying that God celebrates when we return to him.'

Ten minutes to say that? I know Welsh words are longer than English, but still.

The service closes, and we file out quietly. The dog, professional to the last, only makes her first yapping noise as she crosses out into the churchyard.

Her lead tangles around the services noticeboard, still every bit as indecipherable as much of the service, and I decide this was probably an MW, not an AA or HC, because there were no children or wine. I've heard before of newcomers finding services difficult to follow, as if they're in another language. Now I know what that feels like. Even when everyone's lovely, sometimes you need a Bible *and* a phrasebook.

The Vicar is in the doorway, shaking hands with each of us.

'I'm sorry you found us at our Welsh service,' he says to me. 'You don't speak Welsh yourself?'

'I'm afraid not,' I reply. 'My fault. Should have come prepared. Is it always in Welsh?'

'Oh no, we try and keep a balance. Guidelines from on high.'

He means the diocese, not God, and points to a notice on the board behind me. Sure enough, a ten-point dictate states the enforcements of Welsh and English language to have equal weighting in services, newsletters and all parts of church life.

'I see the notice itself is only in English,' I say casually.

The Vicar peers, realises, and mutters to another man, who glares at the offending notice. Action will clearly be taken on this.

I feel bad to have highlighted this, plus like to give my usual contribution to their mission work and utility bills, so I move to the collection pot by the door. Before reaching into my pocket, I know what I've got with me. In my front pocket, nothing but two pence pieces, refused everywhere else. In my back pocket, an envelope stuffed with twenty pound notes.

Exactly what I just put into that pot is between me and God and no one else. The vicar seems happy anyway and waves me off to my journey east.

'Thank you!' he calls cheerily. 'Always nice when a visitor leaves us to the sound of clinking coins!'

4

It's Friday, I'm in Mass

Congregating with Catholics

'And what do *you* do for a living?' I asked the woman in the front row, knowing the answer.

'I'm a vicar,' came her inevitable reply, and for once the giveaway wasn't the outfit. There were three hundred fellow men and women of the cloth here, with more dog collars than on a busy day at Crufts. I was the only unordained person in the room, like the wild uncollared mutt among a group of well-behaved labradors. I could have hid among them and played an ecclesiastical version of 'Where's Wally'.

It felt daunting to address this roomful of professional preachers. No doubt they'd be friendly and supportive, but they'd also be used to public speaking and probably not be afraid of a heckle or two. How do you put down a vicar?[1] Standard putdowns wouldn't work:

'Hey, I don't come to where you work and ... read out the banns of marriage.'
'Yeah, I remember my first ... glass of communion wine.'
'Where'd you learn to whisper, a monastery? ... Oh you did.'

There's a strange occurrence at some church gigs, whereby on any 'dodgier' jokes, the punters look first to the vicar to see if he's laughing. If he is, they might join in. If he's not, they silently agree with him and take against the comedian. We've all been there. You tell a joke at a

---

[1] 'I don't know, how do you put down a vicar?' 'Erm, this should be a punchline.'

church gig that has a keyword like 'sex' or 'Muslim' or 'Pam Rhodes' and you listen out for the collective intake of breath. All eyes will turn to the vicar. He'll give a nervous half-laugh, and then you'll hear an identical half-laugh from everyone else a second later.

I've chatted to Muslim comedians who've found the same thing at mosque gigs, with the attendees checking the imam's degree of laughter first. I mentioned this at a church gig recently and, sure enough, there was that collective intake of breath again.

I feared it could be similar at this clergy conference: surely with the Church of England's hierarchy, all eyes will turn to the bishop? Or at least all the canons will look to the deans, the deans will look to the bishop, and the bishop will look heavenwards before giving a thumbs-up or thumbs-down?

Thankfully, this was not the case. Vicars, it turns out, like to let their hair down. Perhaps because of their position at life's murkier ends – births, deaths, and even marriages – you can detect hints of the dark sense of humour found among doctors, nurses and undertakers. The myth of the humourless vicar *is* just a myth. Most have a keen sense of comedy, as you'll no doubt hear in the jokes at the start of sermons.

Which leads me to my only complaint about the gig. There are gags that comedians do that we're pretty sure will hit big. We call them 'bankers', although since the financial crash, we're considering renaming them to a more, well, bankable profession, like 'AA men' or 'service station toilet attendants who adhere to the sixty-minute toilet-clean countdown'.

Yet the big laughs never came from these vicars, because whenever I did a particularly snappy Bible-based gag that I thought would go down well, they'd all just start scribbling: my jokes, for their sermons.

I know they'd had a day of seminars and were used to note-taking, but these are my gags! They're not sermon fodder. 'Thou shalt not steal,' I believe the Old Testament says quite early on, and quite clearly. And don't tell me 'it's not as if it was set in stone' – it's a commandment, it was set in a very famous stone. So that includes my gags, thanks vicars.

Apart from a few rebukes about gag-thievery, the gig went well. The banter was kept ecclesiastical and I stopped asking people what they did for a living. Well I was going to, until a gaggle of vicars started pointing to a bearded chap, chanting, 'Ask him! Ask him!'

I sighed and asked the question. 'And what do *you* do for a living?' expecting to hear yet another person say, 'Vicar,' followed by three hundred titters.

'I'm the Pope's astronomer,' came the surprising reply.

Now that's an unusual one. Who knew the Pope even had an astronomer? I didn't know that the Vatican had an observatory. It makes you wonder about the other great introductions made by the staff of world leaders:

'How do you do, I'm the presidential osteopath. '

'Nice to meet you, I'm the Dalai Lama's pool cleaner.'

'Oh and have you met the chief canine manicurist to King Harald V of Norway?'

After the show, I chatted with Dr Guy, or the Pope's astronomer as I shall continue to call him, because I just like saying it.[2]

'The Vatican has resources,' the Pope's astronomer told me. 'And meteorites. We've got a lot of meteorites.'

It goes without saying that if you own the Sistine Chapel, you could probably afford a pretty good telescope, and maybe the odd meteorite or two. Guy is one of a team of twelve astronomers to His Holiness.[3]

As you'd expect at a conference of three hundred vicars, he was in high demand for conversation. It's not often you meet someone who's trained as both a priest and a planetary scientist, and made it to the highest position that straddles both jobs.[4]

During our brief chat, he made it clear that his focus was the crossover of the science/faith debate. He spoke of how the two need to work together rather than be competing ends of the spectrum. Presumably then, being the only Catholic in a roomful of Anglicans is the last of his worries. If you can blur the borders between faith and science, you can definitely blur those between Catholic and Protestant.

'If you look up to the stars then ...' He was cut off by an intruding vicar, eager for a meet-and-greet-eorite.

I assume that he was going to say next that if you look up to the

[2] 'The Pope's astronomer' sounds as if it should be a euphemism, to go with, 'Who's "she", the cat's mother?' and 'I'm going to see a man about a dog'.
[3] A reminder that astronomy is not astrology. He's into planets, not horoscopes. Although the Pope does have 12 astronomers, so maybe they double-up with a star sign each. Perhaps His Holiness summons them one by one each morning to tell him that Capricorn Catholics the world over are going to have a lucky day.
[4] Apart from perhaps chaplain to the International Space Station.

stars then you realise that we're all the same. It's quite possible he was going to say, 'If you look up to the stars then you'll see God has spelt out in the night sky the words: "Give up Anglicans, the Catholics are right".' I'll never know.

After all, Catholics are big business ...

Why in Rome?

St Peter died in Rome, and each Pope is his successor. Rome became home to the Catholic Church when it split from the Eastern Orthodox churches in the schism of 1054. Good word, that, 'schism'. Must try and use it more often.

Who in Rome?

There have been more than 260 Popes to date. Not that you should try and date any of them. Just a handful have abdicated, nine were deposed, and more than thirty have had their lives schismed cruelly short. Around a quarter of previous popes have been made saints.

Where in Rome?

The Vatican is both the world's smallest independent state and the least populous, with around eight hundred residents. It has its own helipad, which Pope Benedict XVI was known to use. He actually held a papal pilot's licence, and could often be found schisming the helipopeter from the land.

When in Rome ...

... do as the Roman Catholics do. There are more than a billion Catholics worldwide, and they're growing – not so much to do with conversion but more to do with views on birth control. There is no way to crowbar 'schism' into this sentence.

---

* * *

The morning after meeting the planetary priest, I find myself dwelling on our Catholic cousins. I'm gradually taking the day to reach a less ecclesiastical booking: a pub gig off the M5 that pays little but is always a delight, and most importantly is opposite one of my favourite takeaways. Sometimes that's reason enough to take the gig.

Too often the Protestant/Catholic divide is highlighted, rather than our commonalities. Walking down a busy North Birmingham street on a Friday morning, I'm feeling a kinsmanship with all and any faith group, since within view I can see a mosque, a synagogue, a church and an abbey, plus a brown sign pointing to an Eastern Orthodox church. I'm a Cornishman, so I just need to hear a Devon accent to think somewhere's multicultural. This street is blowing my mind – it must deserve some kind of plaque or government grant.

Keen for some urban exploring, I wait at a pelican crossing with three other gents, who I name John, George and Ringo, on account of this being the 'abbey' road.[5] As we cross, my chosen three don't conform to the single-file choreography I'd hoped for, but I don't cause a fuss. Let it be, I think to myself.

John and George cross straight into the abbey. Ringo doesn't join them, preferring to head down the road towards the mosque. Friday is the holy day for Muslims, but that doesn't mean that the abbey is closed for business – in fact far from it: dozens of people along with John and George are entering for morning mass. I was just going to window shop to let my all-you-can-eat breakfast go down, ahead of my all-you-can-eat pizza buffet at lunchtime, so I decide to join them.

Now, I'm no Catholic. I've only got one sibling, icons are things I double-click on and the only confession I've ever made in a booth was to a passport photo machine about forgetting to shave. I've been to some 'high Anglican' smells-and-bells services in the past – so high that I learnt extra Latin and reeked of incense for days – but I've never actually attended Catholic mass. I'm only 60% sure I'm actually allowed in without a membership card.

I enter anyway, although I don't partake in the entrance customs that John and George do: they dip their hands into some holy water and cross themselves. I decide that the best way to treat this service with respect is to sit, stand, sing and respond *en masse* in mass, but not to join customs that I know little of.

In the abbey itself, I'm hoping to sit on the back pew, but I don't have a choice – we're filled to the rafters with at least two hundred people

[5] It's also the mosque road, but that's not a famous album cover.

here. On a Friday? Have they not got jobs? They can't all be time-filling comedians?

I take the only remaining seat, halfway up the aisle, causing ten people to shuffle along. We instantly stand and everyone but me joins in some responses. Everyone knows exactly what to say. I panic that I was supposed to take a service sheet with what to say written down, but no, no one's got one – all this is from memory. I'm impressed. In the Church of England we need everything printed in bold for us – on a screen or on a pamphlet distributed on the way in, which is either yellow, pink, green or blue, depending on where in the month we are. But here, the gathered worshippers know everything off by heart. Anglicans suddenly look as if we're in a school play, reading our lines from scripts, while Catholics look like the RSC.

The main priest – there are too many priests to count – is an Irishman with bushy eyebrows that are the first thing you see, even from the back pew I'm sure. They'd knock you out in the front row. I wonder which came first: his ordination or the TV show *Father Ted*, because one definitely influenced the other.

The responses continue over several minutes: the priest says something, the congregation respond, sometimes even with movements of hands to the face or chin. I don't even attempt to join in. If there's one thing I advise a first-timer at a Catholic church, it's not to sit at the front. The last thing you want is to look caught out in a game of 'musical chairs' meets 'heads, shoulders, knees and toes'.

Everyone suddenly kneels, so I do too. The collapsing bodies reveal a church that's ornate and artistic, with enough statues to rival Madame Tussauds. They're saints, many of them standing on lions. Impressive, especially if that's an exact representation of how they lived and travelled around.

To an Anglican like me, the only artwork I'm used to seeing is the depiction of Noah's Ark by the Sunday school kids, pinned on a noticeboard that's the church equivalent of a fridge door. Where's our fourteenth-century fresco of Judas' betrayal? This interior is at the same time a church, a museum, an art gallery and a terrifying episode of *Doctor Who*. Protestants have always been wary of anything that might be considered idol worship, so have avoided vivid paintings of the Messiah or ornate sculptures. In our church the crayoned attempts of William aged 9, bless him for trying, are nothing to worship.

Everyone joins in with various Amens and the like, and concludes with a prayer I've heard of: the 'Kyrie Eleison' (the 'Lord, have mercy' prayer, found in non-Catholic churches too). My distant memory knows the name, but I think autocorrected it to 'Kylie Ellison', who my brain wrongly tells me is a famous Catholic.

The Liturgy of the Word follows: a reading. Looking around me, some older worshippers run beads through their hands, as a reminder for prayer – somewhere between an abacus and a prayer to-do list. Everything seems to matter more here. There's an added sense of ceremony to the Protestant equivalents – indeed, many of the attendees would probably not think of non-Catholic communion as anything like an equivalent. Here the whole occasion is steeped in tradition and mystery.

There's no sermon here today – it's a short Friday mass and not a Sunday service. Instead we enter the Liturgy of the Eucharist, as the bread and wine are prepared with more prayer. I'm shown up once more as the obvious non-Catholic, when the Lord's Prayer is spoken and I unknowingly utter aloud, 'For thine is the kingdom, the power and the … oh.' It turns out they don't say that bit here. Some Catholics do nowadays, but it's not reached the abbey yet. Some turn to look at me, turn back, and we all say, 'Amen.'

Then comes the Sign of Peace. I'm used to this in my C of E church – a nice communal moment where we all get to greet each other. I normally reach a few – in front, behind, a keen sidesman – but here it seems customary to greet everyone. If you're near the door, I wouldn't be surprised if you're encouraged out of the building and down the street to knock on a few neighbours' doors to greet them too.

There's a baby with his grandparents in front of me, and having greeted Granny and Granddad, I give a little wave to the baby and say, 'Peace be with you.'

'No,' says Granny sternly. 'Do it properly.'

'I'm sorry?' I'm a little stunned. That can't be in the liturgy. Neither, judging by her look, is waving. Granddad has already moved on to shaking hands with every priest he can reach in time.

'You shake his hand,' she says. 'He wants a proper Peace.'

'Oh, I'm sorry.' I shake his baby hand and give a heartfelt, 'Peace be with you,' as I stare at him. I had always thought general form was to not shake hands with a stranger's baby unless invited, but here the Peace supersedes all social niceties.

'Thank you,' Granny says, and smiles. Not a word of the Peace back from the baby though – just another example of the rude youth of today's broken Britain.

As everyone else turns back to face front, Granddad is the last to sit down. 'Got four of them!' he whispers. Looking up, I see that's only about half of the priests here.

The priest with the eyebrows invites us to sing the 'Agnus Dei', and the moment of transubstantiation occurs, when the bread becomes the body, and the wine becomes the blood. The bread is referred to as 'the host', I now discover – throughout the service I'd assumed they'd been talking about the main priest, as the host of a dinner party or a game show host. I should have realised of course that the host is Jesus – and we're all invited to this feast. You don't even need to bring a bottle.

My invitation though is reliant on me becoming Catholic, so I stay in the pew and send an RSVP heavenward: 'Sorry, but I'll be unable to attend ...'.

Protestant or non-denominational churches I've been to encourage all to partake of communion if you do so at your own church, but I'm aware that the Catholic Church prefers to restrict it to their own. It's quite understandable: if you believe the bread and wine actually becomes Christ, you don't want people like me consuming while denying what they believe. Imagine you've got friends over for Sunday roast. You're serving lamb ...

'Ooh lovely,' the friend says. 'I love Supernoodles.'

'It's not Supernoodles,' you reply. 'It's lamb.'

'Well, "You say potato, I say pot*arto*".'

'No, I say lamb. It's lamb.'

'Well I think it's Supernoodles. But it represents lamb, if that helps. Either way I love it.'

'Put your knife and fork down, and please leave.'

There are a lot of priests here. It looks like last night's vicar convention. There's Father Eyebrows of course, but supporting him is a deacon, a crucifier (which is not someone who crucifies, I'm happy to say, but someone who carries the cross), a thurifier (who carries the thurible, as I'm sure you know), and other assorted altar servers. One effect is that the two hundred congregants process, receive and recess in record time. It must be three minutes, tops. It's the perfect combination of a ton of priests and a regular congregation who have done this a thousand times.

The priests recess down the aisle, and the people leave slowly, taking time to cross themselves, kiss the statues, and dip in the holy water.[6] Some light candles as they go, including Granny from earlier.

Granddad mumbles as he pushes the pushchair out. 'But you lit one of those yesterday.' She tuts and follows them.

Ritual is embraced by this abbey family. It's not in vogue in many modern churches; the notion of repeating the same movements and mantras repels some. The numbers here today though would be the envy of many churches, especially on a Friday morning, so there must be something significant happening here.

Catholicism is of course more genetic than some strands of Christianity, but this only means that the Catholic Church will be alive and kicking long after other maverick churches have become trendy bars. My Anglican vicar once told me that one thing he loves about our church is the continuity: that people have worshipped there every Sunday for seven hundred years. Through wars and umpteen monarchs, the people have come to give thanks and pray for help.

Part of the mystery of Christianity is that Jesus can be fully God and fully human, and in touring around churches, some seem godly to me, and others seem human. This abbey today had the grandeur, the vaulted ceilings and the ornate attention to detail that points upwards. If I'm honest, I don't feel that so much in some modern churches. There I see coffee cups, toddler groups, and a general clamour of people: a good dose of ground-level humanity. Both are vital. It seems some churches are for washing your hands (literally, for the Catholics I saw here), and some churches are for getting your hands dirty.

That's not to say that huge and ancient buildings have no humanity – far from it. From large organisations like the Catholic Worker Movement, to nunneries and hospices, large archaic buildings like this have held people who have done great things at a personal level. The Catholic Worker was pioneered a hundred years ago by Dorothy Day and Peter Maurin, showing anti-war, anti-discrimination and social justice to be Christian and Catholic themes.

[6] Just their fingers – not a full body dip.

These good people are easily forgotten, especially by the secular world. I know many comedians and others alike who would hear the word 'Catholic' and think only of anti-abortion, anti-contraception and cover-ups. The Catholic Church has got a bad reputation in the big wide world.

I see a Church full of good people, with, yes, some bad apples that are rotten to the core. Those who covered up and put the bad apples back on the shelf are culpable too of course, but the danger is then that the entire institution is pilloried. The same happens whether it's the Catholic Church or the BBC – those who are against such institutions throw everything at them. They must look inward and ensure that such things can never happen again and then, hopefully, they can move on.

I would urge people to look beyond the stereotypes and guessing games. Yes there are wrongdoers, but I've seen generous, holy people committed to God and committed to a life of charity, and they should be more visible. In the meantime the Catholic Church may take some years to shake off its bad press among the unchurched, but then that's something it knows a lot about: penance.

5

A Coventry Carol

Seeking Salvation Army

'Twas the week before Christmas, and all through the land,
All the clubs were a-thrivin', and work dos were planned.
Cabbies and shoppers drove their cars over salt,
And in Coventry outskirts, I ground to a halt.

I was here for the weekend, for three days of shows
Bringing 'Ha ha ha ha's, plus some 'Ho ho ho's.
The audience at Christmas are an unruly bunch:
Mostly work parties who have been drinking since lunch.

While the Edinburgh Festival gives creative fun summers,
December's our penance: gigs of ninety-odd plumbers.
There's heckling and boozing, and free Santa hats
And through each performance, the loudest of chats.

This club wasn't central but out in the sticks:
An industrial park just off the M6.
Our hotel was in need of a nice lick of paint.
I won't say its name, though I 'lodged' a complaint.

But parking was ample, and between every show
I could drive somewhere else ... if it weren't for the snow.
For as I arrived, the ice started forming
And the cold winter sun didn't do any warming.

So my weekend was stuck here – sounds pretty rough, eh?
A Burger King, Tesco, a Pizza Hut buffet,
Then Laserquest, bowling, an attempt at Tex-Mex,
And a digital ten-screen deluxe multiplex.

So Tesco provided all presents that year:
F&F clothing, cheap chocolates, cheap beer.
And after my shopping, to screen number eight,
With Vince Vaughn in Lapland I'd now hibernate.

The cinema warmed but the movie was rough
And credits soon rolled, just not soon enough.
Before heading outside to see new snow a-falling,
I made for the Gents, because nature was calling.

It was totally empty, being Thursday, four-thirty.
So I went for a cubicle once I found one not dirty.
The main door then opened and in burst a fellow,
And through my loo door, I heard him say 'Hello?'

I like to be friendly; I hate being mean.
But this wasn't the place, with a door in-between.
'Hello?!' he repeated, with minimal tact,
Which left me a quandary: do I say hello back?

Or do I ignore him, which doesn't seem right?
I'm British (reserved), yet British (polite).
Politeness won out, so I answered, quite shocked.
'Hello?' I exclaimed, glad the loo door was locked.

Cubicles vacant, he was spoilt for choice,
And I knew no one here, let alone knew the voice.
So why was he talking? We all know the code.
You don't speak to strangers while on the commode.

'So what are you doing?' He continued to speak!
Do I answer again, though I'm feeling quite meek?
Do I give him a number, a 'one' or a 'two'?
How can I get him to leave me and my loo?

I ought to reply to his question, I reckoned,
So I said, 'Nearly out, just give me a second!'
I wished I could vanish, prevent our confronting.
But then I was curious to what he was wanting.

Maybe a cubicle's what he desired,
But with four others empty, that thought soon expired.
Perhaps he left something before in this stall?
But no, nothing here, even ... oh. No loo roll.

'Get a move on!' he said, as I imagined him pacing.
Enough then, I thought – I'm going out to face him.
I eased back the lock and it turned from 'Engaged'
Back to 'Vacant', and I readied to see him, enraged.

I creaked my door open in order to finally
Glimpse the strange man ... who was at the urinal. He
Hadn't been barking at my toilet door:
He was standing just near it and I instantly saw

Why he'd uttered such strangeness, because I hadn't known
That all of this time he'd just been on the phone.
'Hello ... What you doing...' he'd said to his mate ...
'Get a move on!': He'd phoned him because he was late!

His chat hadn't been aimed at me, like I'd feared
He was just unhygienic, not overly weird.
I moved to the sinks, both relieved and 'relieved',
But he was still glaring, I'm sure I perceived.

'Course while he'd been checking his friend's whereabouts,
I'd answered him back from the loo with my shouts.
He wasn't the weird one, like I'd thought inside.
No, *I* was the weird one, cos I had replied.

I had to save face, so cool as a cat
I sneaked phone to ear, and continued my chat.
'Yeah, watching a film,' I said to my phone,
Pretending I wasn't just talking alone.

That would explain why I'd seemed to reply.
'Good movie,' I told my fake friend (one more lie).
Cos there wasn't a friend and the film had been bad,
But at least he'd not think I was stark raving mad.

And so there we stood, two phone-calls a-taking,
One of us real, the other one faking.
Then all of a sudden while I spoke to fake mate,
I felt in my hand my phone start to vibrate.

Quick as a flash, before ringtone alerted,
I swiftly pressed 'cancel': call and problem diverted.
The chap hadn't noticed – I could finally relax,
So I left for the foyer, hearing festive soundtracks.

Kirsty MacColl serenaded The Pogues
As the door to the gents pneumatically closed.
But slowness to close meant sounds weren't just musical;
Also I heard, 'There was this bloke in a cubicle,

He was having a chat on the phone while he sat!
Disgusting, I tell you – how filthy is that?!'
The door simply closed, I heard no more talk,
And Kirsty and Shane sang of choirs in New York.

So next time a stranger says 'Hi', do not spoil it,
Whether you meet in a street, lift or a toilet;
Respond at your peril: without further ado
He'll be telling his mate that you phone on the loo.

* * *

'Twas a few minutes later, and I trudged through the snow
With still several hours until my next show.
The other comedians had said, 'Let's get food!'
I'd had buffet and popcorn, but a 'no' would be rude.

So I crossed the white car park, and my pizza I planned,
When I heard unmistakeable sounds: a brass band.
I dwelt more on toppings, on ham, and salami,
And then there were: the Salvation Army.

Cold, bold as brass: a trombone and a tuba.
Each puffed with chilled air like a sub-aqua scuba.
A flugelhorn, tenor horn – a midwinter's dream –
And a cornet: the instrument, not full of ice cream.

The band were in uniform, all upright and dapper.
As they drew to a close, I was the lone clapper.
They nodded a thank you and stopped for a rest,
And some now regretted not wearing a vest.

I engaged the trombonist in some light conversation,
Wondering what links brass bands to salvation.
'It goes back to our founder, one William Booth.
He'd take to the streets, not just to preach truth,

But largely to help folks, in practical ways,
So he'd focus on addicts, the poor, waifs and strays:
The 'undesirables' not welcomed in church.
So he'd go sit with them, not high on a perch.

Booth and wife Catherine, they'd go and they'd listen,
And they founded this group called the East London Mission.
The daughter of William then moved to the States;
Her wagon would transport inebriates

To refuges, to stop guzzling ale by the flagon,
And hence the expression we use: "on the wagon".'
'I didn't know that,' said I to trombonist,
'So is there a link between brass bands and homeless?'

'Well, yes,' he replied. 'See, the Booths preached no booze,
And the old Sally Army would steal the pubs' queues.
Landlords weren't happy with custom less merry
So to bring down the tension, one night in Salisbury,

Charles Fry and his sons had a brainwave: try music.
Because each had an instrument, and knew how to use it.
They just started playing, the rowdy crowds calmed.
Cos we all love a sing-song, even when armed.

Booth said, on hearing how music communes,
'Why should the devil have all the best tunes?'
It seemed rather apt hearing tales of sobriety,
With a boozy gig later, I had cause for anxiety.

It's good that at Christmas, among the beer barrels,
The Salvation Army continue with carols,
But also their work that's often not seen:
Helping the homeless get fed or get clean.

The three things you get from this Santa's grotto
Is 'soup, soap, salvation!' – so goes their old motto.
He asks me the time, saying, 'Well it's quite cold,
And we're due to be finished by now, we were told.

'I don't mind of course, but my horn-playing friend,
She's off to the cinema, might catch the film's end.
Her boyfriend's been phoning, the movie's commenced ...'
At this point, I panicked. Was it him in the Gents?

I made my excuses, thought best not find out
If I've met her boyfriend and his toiletary shout.
So I left them to choose which song to play last
As I dashed away, dashed away, dashed away fast.

The dinner was pleasant, the gig full of cheer,
And now I head south to the sound of Chris Rea.
As I drive home for Christmas, here's that old sound bite:
A Happy Christmas to all, and to all a goodnight!

6

Snow Joke

Kneeling with Neo-Charismatics

I have mixed feelings about snow.

The day of expectation is exciting, when it doesn't quite snow but we're told it might. The day of wonder is magical, when it does fall and we stand at the window singing Dean Martin and judging, 'It might settle, it might you know,' like we know what we're talking about. The day of play is a delight, when we wish we'd bought a sledge and instead rush outside with a tray from the kitchen.

The dog days of snow are less thrilling. It either persists and we panic about being snowed in: newspapers report Snowmageddon, and shops run out of bread so we resort to fruitloaf or crumpets. Or it turns to slush and your dad phones about what a death trap the roads are, and did you ever buy that rock salt he recommended.

By January's second week of this, the word 'York' had been staring up from my diary for some time, more of a threat than a promise of work. It had the menace of a gangster: 'Heating on full, is it? You want to pay those bills, you get up that M1 if you know what's good for you.'

The M1 is surely so named because like the number, it boringly goes straight up with all the swervy exciting bits to its left. The road is long, and maybe the odd winding turn might brighten things up a bit. It's not anyone's favourite motorway (that's the M40), it doesn't contain anyone's favourite services (that's Alderley Edge in Cheshire — a lake and a farm shop!), but it does get you from A to B — or more precisely from the A406 to the B6157.

In bad weather you want local work, or even no work at all. It's not the time to cross the country, changing accent zones at every service station. 'Easy in the snow, guv,' gives way to, 'Look after yerself, m'duck,' and eventually, 'Fettle ye careful-like on t'roads'.

The Met Office journey-o-meter had its needle pointing to 'essential only'. Did a two-hundred-pound gig in York count as essential? It was bill-paying work, so I guessed yes. On the comedy circuit, three or four times a week you ask yourself, is it worth the travel for that money? My old housemate Danny, also a comic, used to put it like this: If you told a non-performer that you'd left an envelope for them containing a couple of hundred pounds in a bar, a five-hour drive away, would they bother to go and get it? Maybe, maybe not. Comics not only decide yes, I will go, but when there we'll spend half an hour trying to get the attention of a roomful of strangers. Odd.

I set off early on the Saturday to face the best chance with the weather. The snow had cleared a little around my house, but then Surrey is nearer the equator than York. As I applied the hand brake in the fast lane of the motorway, I knew it was going to be a long journey.

I, like a lot of comics (and I'm sure circus performers, travelling salesmen and any other hard-to-insure working drivers), have person-alised my driving experience in an individual, yet I'm sure, quite pathetic way. If you spend so much time in your car, you have to. I know a comedian with a shoebox under his passenger seat full of favourite sweets, a toothbrush and a change of underwear. I've passengered in cars where the back seat has been stocked full of crisp packets, novels and Diet Cokes. One comic I know never travels more than two hours without an apple, an orange and a banana on his passenger seat, to halt his temptation for road snacks and fast food. We all perform a sort of geeky, comfortable version of Pimp My Car Interior.

Allow me to introduce you to the Kerensamobile ...

- My Satnav has been programmed to moo like a cow whenever I'm within five miles of a Harvester. Chain restaurants provide the best mix, I find, of value for money and staff who'll leave you alone for three hours while you write jokes on a laptop, plus unlimited visits to the salad cart.
- In the pocket behind the passenger seat – easy reaching while driving – you'll find energy drinks and bottles of Actimel (winter only, to keep them fridge-cold).

- Between front seats, in the container for change or keys or no one knows what, you'll find Polos, TicTacs *and* Softmints, because you never know what mint you'll be in the mood for.
- My glove compartment has last year's edition of the National Trust handbook (because this year's is always in the house).
- The iPod is chock-full of cheesy 1980s power ballads – often marketed as 'Drivetime' by the music PR people, but called 'Porous' by me, on account of it being very soft rock.

Prising myself away from the M25, I worked out that it would have been quicker to walk this far. The M1 felt like a giant step nearer my destination. I was glad that I'd planned ahead to book a hotel for the night. After some faraway gigs I'd gladly turn around and drive straight home, but not tonight. Tonight I looked forward to a midnight welcome at the finest M1 Travelodge that nineteen pounds could buy.

When people think of the job of comedian being a lonely one, this is the nub of it. The long commute, the late night check-in, sometimes feeling like you're the only car on the motorway at 2 a.m. on a Tuesday. The shows are social enough – the circuit provides you with a thousand friends and colleagues you get to know over the years. The onstage part of the job is an odd mix of highly social and yet incredibly isolating, spending half an hour with a hundred new acquaintances, spilling personal stories and spinning yarns so you feel you know each other in a fake, fleeting way. The time spent at home can be nicely social – yes the joke-writing is done alone at a computer, but there's a good deal of tea-making and joke-testing on friends and unfortunate cold-callers. However, solitary travel is loneliness incarnate.

My car eventually crawled past Leicester. I looked at the clock. Still four hours till stage time, but at this rate I'd need every minute. The thought occurred that at this moment, a Yorkshire comedian was probably making the exact opposite journey to Surrey for a gig. I briefly considered designing a website where comedians could enter their upcoming gigs and swap them to avoid ridiculous trips like this.

The brake lights in front suddenly lit up, and it took a second to realise that was my cue to do likewise. I braked, the other car skidded, and I went to brake harder.

As I pressed my foot down, the words of my dad reverberated around my head ...

'Son ... Son ...'

'Get to the point, Dad! I've got some braking to do.'

'Don't brake hard on ice!'

'You could have led with that!'

I caught my foot just in time and turned it into a light braking, then swerved to avoid the zigzagging car before me.

'Oh, and don't turn too hard on ice.'

'Good point.'

My swerve became a gentle nudge of a turn, and Dad's voice went quiet, which presumably meant any collision was avoided for the moment.

Skilfully, I thought, I rounded the car in front, which ground to a halt on the hard shoulder. I tried not to get too smug in case it was me next, but at the same time I felt a bit like Jensen Button.

I remembered my only breakdown call-out to date, which occurred not far from this very spot. A quirk of driving for a living is that I'm stingy when it comes to petrol, and I'll gladly drive well out of my way for fuel that's a penny or two cheaper per litre. On this past occasion I had scowled at the roadside services, with their crazy motorway mark-up. I'd planned to stop at a sneaky supermarket and fill up for at least 2% cheaper. Sadly my ambitions had exceeded the fuel capacity, and the car shuddered to a halt. I realised I'd have to call the RAC and tell them I'd run out of petrol. It was going to be humiliating.

I sensed the patronising tone of the operator's voice, but it was a relief that it was less 'You're the first idiot to do this' and more 'We've got another one'.

After a relatively brief wait (I expected to be in the 'eight hours minimum' category), a geezer of an RAC man appeared and tried to hide his smirk as I needlessly explained the problem of the petrol needle on the dash pointing at the E instead of the F.

His solution was surprisingly old-fashioned – he just sold me some fuel for a fiver. It wouldn't get me far, but the nearest services would do. I promised I'd go straight there, kicking myself that I'd have to pay motorway prices after all.

The most embarrassing exchange took place as the Knight of the Road started back down the hard shoulder to his orange steed.

'Are you okay to rejoin?' he asked.

'Oh, I certainly will,' I said. 'End of the year, I'm signing straight up again, don't you worry about it. You guys are great.'

Finally the smirk that he'd been burying for ten minutes spread across his laddish face. 'No, mate. Are you okay to rejoin the motorway?'

He wasn't soliciting for my membership renewal; he was looking out for my wellbeing. Well, not any more. He just walked away shaking his head.

'What a muppet!' I heard in the distance, or it may have been the wind. It may be unprofessional of a company to call a customer a muppet, but even I could see that he was entirely correct, and fair play to him for not saying it sooner.

I replayed this experience in my head as I approached Donington Park services and promptly pulled in for petrol.

'Rough night out there,' said the assistant, taking my loyalty card.

'Yeah,' I replied. 'I've got to get to York.'

'York? Couple of hours yet, on a good day. And that's not today.'

It's never ideal to have the audience endure an hour-long interval while waiting for an act, but it happens all the time thanks to poor traffic, or alarmingly frequently, comedians just forgetting and staying at home.

Staying at home – that would have been an idea. I slid back to my car with a sandwich, gliding like a Dementor on his lunch break. I made the customary phone call to the venue, which went straight to voicemail.

'I'm en route!' I shouted through a sandwich and my car hands-free kit, skidding across the forecourt. 'Bit behind schedule. It's quite icy!'

I hung up realising they probably knew that. York's not that tropical.

The snow started falling again near Doncaster, about an hour from York. It didn't affect this journey, but you could tell it would affect the post-Travelodge return tomorrow: this was settling snow. The only difference now was the illusion of being in *Star Wars*, driving at warp speed as snowflakes whizzed over the windscreen.[1] Every few minutes

[1] I know 'warp speed' is from *Star Trek*, not *Star Wars*, and that this may annoy purists. So, well spotted. You've passed the Klingon test, now accept your award from Princess Leia.

a voice in your head shouts, 'You're flying the Millennium Falcon! Yes! You're Han Solo!' Then you see no Wookie next to you and remember it's a Nissan Note.

Amazingly, I entered the outskirts of York just a few minutes behind schedule. I easily navigated my way through the central streets, as most sensible people had rightly decided to stay at home. Not me, I'd heard the warnings and thought, 'No. The people of York demand comedy, and it may take me eight hours of driving and a few risky manoeuvres, but I'm going to give it to them. Because I value their entertainment, and more importantly because that nineteen pound Travelodge room is non-refundable.'

I phoned the venue again – still voicemail. 'I'm coming!' I steered around an old man walking his dog into the road, none of us able to tell where the pavement ended and the street began. Mad dogs and Englishmen go out in the bleak midwinter.

Parking in deep snow is surprisingly easy – you just stop the car anywhere and assume it's free parking. So for all I knew, I'd left my car in the middle of a roundabout.

I ran through the three-inch snow, rucksack on shoulder, socks sopping. Ahead of me I could see the inviting lights of the bar. Even the dingiest bar looks welcoming when all around is frosty. A glance at my watch told me I was due onstage any second, if their show timings had gone to plan.

'I'm here for the show!' I panted at the barman. My inner Anneka Rice yelled, 'Stop the clock!'[2]

'What show?' replied the barman. His words and demeanour removed all thoughts of this as a welcoming bar.

'The comedy show. The stand-up.'

'Oh, that's been cancelled. Not enough interest.'

This was not good news. I dropped my bag to the floor with a crash. 'I'm one of the acts!'

'So? It's still cancelled.' He stepped away to serve someone else, but I couldn't let it stop there. I realised that sometimes on the night an audience just doesn't show, but I needed more clarification than this.

'When did you pull it then?' I asked. If it was ten minutes ago, that's not quite so annoying. If it was an hour ago, I could have turned around

---

[2] Anyone old enough to remember *Treasure Hunt* has one.

at Doncaster, or at least not endured running late on black ice, i.e. driving, as slowly as possible, as quickly as possible.

'Er, Tuesday I think,' came the sullen reply.

'WHHHAT?!' I exclaimed. 'Five days ago?'

'Numbers were slow. I think people didn't want to travel in the snow.'

Too right they didn't. I certainly didn't. I'd spent ten hours in the car that day, at speeds reminiscent of a cross-country milk round. If I've travelled through seven accent zones, punters from York's suburbs could have made the effort, surely.

The barman's laidback response, and most crucially the overwhelming lack of an apology or explanation, made me think he just didn't get it. Like some of the roads I'd endured, I really needed closure.

'I'm not local, you know! I've travelled from Surrey. In that weather!' I gestured out of the window, through four dabs of Blu-Tack, which probably once held a poster declaring 'Comedy!' with a picture of my face. That poster was no longer there, and I wished I wasn't either.

The barman sniffed. 'Oh. Well the manager's not here tonight. He's the one who made the call.'

I just wish he *had* made the call to me on Tuesday. I'd have had a nice week knowing the only journey I'd make on Saturday would be to the kitchen for a mug of Whittard's Dreamtime.

'Well can you get him on the phone?' I demanded. I don't know why – he'd just repeat what this most unwelcome of gig guardians had said. I just wanted to hear the word 'Sorry' or 'Whoops'. Even laughing in my face would have acknowledged that the trip hadn't been easy.

'Oh, I don't know his number.'

'So what do I do now? Just go home. Another ten hours?'

'Yeah I guess,' he said as he finally left to take the drinks order from an increasingly impatient customer.

Oh, the customer can wait all night. I've waited ten hours in the car for a bit of stage time and some cash. Which reminded me ...

'What about my pay?!' I exclaimed across the bar.

'Not my area, mate,' came the reply mid-pour. 'Mark's the manager. Back Monday.'

'I live in Surrey!' I repeated. 'I'm not here on Monday! I shouldn't be here now! I should be at home watching it snowing rather than driving in it!'

I gave up on getting a sensible reply from my pint-pulling nemesis. He knew nothing, either about the so-called gig, or about common decency and how to deal with people, people who might be a little stressed after an arduous commute to a job that doesn't exist.

I unearthed my phone from four layers of clothing and dialled the number I'd called en route. In the back office I heard a phone ring, duly ignored by this enemy of entertainment, clearly the only barman on duty. It scared me that he was responsible for the entire pub. Woe betide if the log fire got out of hand – he'd have his arms folded muttering, 'Mark the manager deals with all health and safety issues.'

My earlier voicemails had clearly hit this communications cul-de-sac. I ransacked my phone for another number: the booker.

'He——o?' it crackled.

'Steve? It's Paul! Paul Kerensa!'

'Can't quite—you!? I'm in Denmark!' came the tinny voice through the phone.

'This gig! In York! I'm here but it's not on. They pulled it days ago!'

'Oh. I've been i—enmark!'

We exchanged more noises across the North Sea. It became clear that Steve the absent promoter had left the running of the gig in the incapable hands of Mark the absent manager, who had left the pub in the incompetent hands of a sadly present barman. I explained to Steve in broken syllables just how bad the snow had been, how long the journey had been, and how sure he could be that I was going to get paid in full for this. Thankfully Steve was also a performer, who had probably done his fair share of long drives for cancelled gigs, so he was quick to agree that the cheque would indeed be in the post. I trusted Steve. Otherwise I'd be looking at staging some kind of sit-in. Given the weather outside, I was tempted to stage one anyway.

But why waste any more time here, I thought? If I was being paid anyway, then I'd just been sent home early. I had become the precise example that my housemate Danny had described: of a long drive across the country to pick up an envelope of cash and come home again.

My journey home of course wouldn't be until the next day, since I had the bright lights[3] of Travelodge waiting for me a few miles back down the motorway. So after a last sneering look to the barman, I bade farewell

---

[3] So bright. Why have LED bedside lamps?

to York city centre, turned on the iPod and motored back down the long road. Dean Martin and I sang about the weather outside. It was indeed frightful.

* * *

Only a minimal dusting of snow overnight thankfully, so I easily spot my car in the white blanket of a car park. It's got a thin white hat now, but with a bright blue January sky above us, the sun promises a good defrosting to help me on my way this Sunday morning. It's a four-hour journey home at best, so I'm stopping an hour or so into it at a church I've found online. Yes I'm partly using their church service as a motorway service, but I think that's allowed. It looks lively and promises a creative, contemporary approach, as well as a pre-service hot beverage. That's the clincher for me when comparing it with one down the road that, just judging by the photos online, looks like a bigger, colder building, with no guarantees of coffee. Mine has a nice low ceiling and lots of radiators. I get neo-charismatic evangelical vibes from their website, as well as their postcode. I think it means they sing loudly and occasionally put their hands in the air. I'm an Anglican. We only put our hands in the air to tell the vicar his microphone's off.[4] I head south once more.

My satnav delivers me to the door of what looks less like a church building and more like a warehouse on an industrial estate, largely because it is a warehouse on an industrial estate. Most of the units are closed for the weekend, but one buzzes with noise as I drive up – there's no doubting this is it. Even with the car windows closed, I can hear the hum of music fade in as I approach.

I park and tentatively approach the warehouse of noise, like it's a speakeasy in the 1930s. You'd think you'd need a password, but for the friendly team on the door offering leaflets and smiles.

I follow one snowy family through the doors, and once inside coffee greets me like an old friend. It's so refreshing to find hot drinks before the service – surely a cold Sunday start, pre-sermon, is just when you need the caffeine? Most places only have coffee as a reward at the end of it.

The room is wide, with maybe two hundred seats, mostly full. The

---

[4] Or sometimes we don't tell him.

cold morning hasn't put off this crowd. In fact they're revelling in the chilly weather – the giant doormat is soggy with boot-shaken snow, and every entrant is rosy-cheeked and beaming about the weather. Clearly they haven't got a three-hour drive home ahead of them.

I make a conscious decision to put aside my narkedness at my long pointless trip, and take my coffee to a comfy seat over to one side. Once the locals are through the door and shed of their coats, quite a few come to greet me, which is nice. I explain to each that I'm just visiting, mainly to encourage them to focus on newbies with a real chance of returning, but that doesn't dissuade many from starting up conversations. Kids tell me of yesterday's impromptu sledging championships, and adults tell me of yesterday's trip to A&E.

The service doesn't so much start as ease in gently. The band has been playing throughout, segueing from tuning up to warming up to backing music, and now the audience starts joining in with familiar songs. I know it's a congregation, not an audience, but with a ten-piece band on a giant stage with no altar, this looks more like a music gig than any church service I've been to. At least at their gig they've managed to pull a crowd – more than can be said of York's Comedy Pod. It's telling that this church has its own record label, and I can see, and hear, why.

Almost on the dot of 10.30 a.m., the worship leader finishes one song and most of the people applaud, while still sitting. So now we're in service time, we're asked to stand, and the music moves up a notch. More people join the band, and words are now displayed on the screen rather than leaving us to remember or guess the lyrics.

The mass of sound from the stage – and warmth from the radiators – means we forget about the icy morning, and within seconds it's like we're mid-service. Hands are aloft, flags are being waved at the side of the stage: the worship's gone to a hundred miles per hour in three seconds flat. The singing though is anything but flat – this several hundred strong crowd can sure hold a tune. It's like the atmospheric effect of a football ground – the greater the number of singers, the more the duff notes are levelled out. We're packed full here this morning, and what singing you can hear over the electric guitar riffs sounds great. The guitarists take centre stage, meaning the poor harpist at the back has lugged her instrument all through the snow to be unfortunately drowned out, but I focus and almost convince myself I can hear the occasional pling-pling.

Modern hymn gives way to rock anthem, rock anthem gives way to contemplative worship.[5] Between most songs there are several minutes of 'singing in tongues': the band play without vocals and some of the people let the Spirit guide their voices. It actually sounds quite beautiful – it so easily could not, given that two hundred people appear to be picking random notes. As a dyed-in-the-wool, stuck-in-the-mud, cucumber-sandwich-in-the-rectory-garden Anglican, I mostly just stay quiet. I know my time to sing, and it's when those words appear on the screen. It was a big enough jump for us traditional C of E types to go from holding a leather-bound copy of *Hymns Ancient & Modern* to looking up at a projector screen. I remember distinctly thinking, 'No book to hold? But what do we do with our hands?'

Well, this lot are showing me what to do with them – raise them. There's some serious lactic acid building up around here. While the people either side of me are nearly touching the roof, I make do with hands to shoulder height. That's extreme enough for me for one day.

I'm hearing babbling from my left and babbling from my right, as the music continues to play underneath. Shall I give it a go? How do you start? Am I meant to wait for the Spirit to give me some syllables to sing, or at least count me in? I scavenge my brain for a divine voice saying, 'A one, a two, a one, two, three, four …' but can't hear one. So I decide to just go for it. I, Paul Kerensa, Anglican, am going to musically ad-lib. Here goes …

The band stop. I just let out a 'Laaa!' and receive a few looks. Most don't notice, thankfully, since they're all bringing their lyrical offerings to a close.

The minister has taken to the stage and reads us some words of encouragement from Ephesians. I like that he's reading it from a Bible – it unsettles me, needlessly, when I hear leaders just quote large passages verbatim. Show me the book you're reading from. It tells me you haven't made it up.[6]

He requests us to sit. There are some light-hearted jokes at the expense of the icy weather, and I quickly clock that this speaker is a natural when it comes to a room this size. I don't know whether this

[5] i.e. I can hear the harp.
[6] Atheist readers may be thinking, 'Well they did make it up …'. To you, dear atheist reader, I say: I applaud you for getting this far. Hopefully by the end you won't be thinking, 'Is he going to visit another church?' Because yes, I am.

church is charismatic, but he certainly is. He's Barack Obama with a Midlands accent.

I can see why this congregation is so full, especially of younger people. The leadership seems very accessible, the welcomes are genuine, and according to the announcements from the front, I've just missed their Christmas services featuring live animals. Apparently the kids loved it; the cleaners less so. It's never said what animals they were, so I assume it was probably a donkey and maybe a sheep. I have heard of churches having camels. For all I know though it could have been a lizard and a walrus, or maybe it was just an unplanned intrusion by a local Jack Russell. Perhaps there was just a window open and a few wasps flew in.[7]

Just as everyone's finally found their seats, the minister calls a comfort break. I don't think I've been to a church with an interval like this before (and I've been to a three-hour Catholic service). I turn to the neighbour to my left. I wouldn't normally start the conversation, but one question is burning away. 'So what animals did you have at Christmas?'

He looks confused by my question. 'Turkey,' he replies.

I actually meant whether the Christmas service had featured a donkey, but don't persist in my questioning. We exchange pleasantries, and he queries how I'm so far from home, given the state of the roads.

'I'm a stand-up comedian,' I explain.

'Oh, right,' he says. It makes sense to him now why I make stupid journeys: I have a stupid job. 'So you were performing somewhere last night?'

'York,' I reply. Please don't ask anything about the gig.

'Many in the audience on a night like it was?'

'No, just me,' I tell him. He looks confused and heads off for a coffee refill.

When we're all resettled with drinks, the minister embarks on an epic sermon: forty minutes of vivacious, energetic preaching. I'm impressed at hearing a relaxed, funny talk, which keeps returning to biblical passages for support, with calls for us to transform ourselves and our society. Yet at the same time there's no 'us and them'. This is a church that goes out of its way to welcome everyone, and not judge. We're reminded that we all fall short, and we all pick ourselves up. I hear

---

[7] Silly thoughts: there are no wasps in December.

the occasional 'Amen' ad-libbed from the crowd after particularly salient points, and by the end I'm inclined to join in. I don't of course – it's not written on the screen for me.

The big push at the end of the talk is for us to get right with God, that no human or church is in a position to judge – we alone need to have some one-to-one with the Almighty, and so prayer time is a big deal in this church. We spend a good twenty minutes in informal prayer, with music underneath, prayer both out loud and unspoken, and the occasional public one shared from the front. There's a proper altar call for those who want their lives transformed, even though there's no altar. Several people make amends with the Lord in this time, and it feels very powerful.

'Are you going up?' asks the man next to me.

'Er, no, I don't think so,' I say. Is that the right answer? It was a great sermon, but I thought he was calling up people to make a once-in-a-lifetime change to their lives. Apparently not.

'No, I might not this week,' he says. 'I go up most weeks.'

'You're transformed every week?!' I ask.

'Not every week, no. It's been a quiet few days.'

I'm genuinely not sure whether I misunderstood who the altar call was calling, or whether this man just has a wild time from Monday to Saturday and turns back to Christ every seventh day. I feel perhaps it's somewhere between the two – maybe in this church the altar call is more akin to Catholic confession than I realised, where each week you can come and lay bare your weekly sins, rather than it being a once-in-a-blue-moon dramatic rebirth. Maybe when they turn to Christ, it's less a hundred-and-eighty-degree turn, and more just a few degrees – a turn that just puts us back on kilter. In that way, turns aren't one-offs, but regular updates to nudge us a few degrees back on track, like a ship tweaking its steering ever so slightly. The sea looks clear, but stay on your current course and in a few hundred miles there's a massive iceberg over that horizon.

This service ends as it began – not with a sudden start/stop, but with a fade. The band continue quietly strumming guitars and loudly strumming harps, the prayers continue, and I opt not to wait it out till the conclusion – we've been given our final blessing and permission to depart, so I decide to hit the road. I've had my post-service coffee before we started, and I've got three hours to drive on sodden snow.

The sun has been shining throughout, and my car and the roads are nicely defrosting. I leave the icy car park of the industrial estate with care, making some of those fractional half-a-degree turns that I was just considering in the service.

The lonely part of stand-up is the drive, but the warm welcome at places like this warehouse church make up for that, even when the gig never happened. The thought gets me mentally checking my upcoming gigs: next is Hull in a few days. Best double-check with the venue that it's not been cancelled, because much as I like the M1, it's no M40.

Devon is a Place on Earth

Rogating with rural Anglicans

After a five minute parking session to get as close to the stone wall as possible, I pull on the handbrake. Narrow as these country lanes are, numerous tractors, 4x4s and landing craft are going boot-to-pedal up these hills, covered in dents and scratched paint. I don't fancy bits of my car living out their days stuck to a farm vehicle in south Devon. Once again, I am in search of a church.

'How am I going to get out?' asks my better half Zoë, from the passenger seat.

We are in search of a church. As if I am an expert, I talk her through tips for visiting a new church, as she clambers over the handbrake.

'Yeah, if you're just nice to the greeters and take a seat near the back they'll stop any staring soon enough.'

We look up and see a gaggle of churchgoers stare at us: a man dragging a woman across the front seats of a Nissan.

'Morning!' we both say chirpily.

We follow them in the cool, spring sunshine to a beautiful spired building we spied on day one of our holiday. It is at the centre of the village, yet still overlooking the sea thanks to the village's hilltop placement. This is from an age where villages were built around the churches. God's got the best views, and the vicar here's got the second best.

The noticeboard outside tells us the usual details of name of church, service times, and vicar's phone number – the ecclesiastical equivalent of 'The Church of England welcomes careful parishioners – please worship responsibly'. A printed A4 piece of paper has been taped on top: 'Rogation Sunday'.

Zoë and I look at each other and shrug. Rogation Sunday is a new one on us.

Some traditional days from the Church calendar

- Trinity Sunday: The Sunday after Pentecost.
- Quadragesima Sunday: The Sunday after Ash Wednesday, clearly something to do with quad bikes and drag racing.
- Spacehopper Club Sunday: The Sunday after the church has been used as a playgroup all summer, and the kids want to apologise for the mess.
- Rogation Sunday: Pass. Hopefully we'll find out.

'Is it "rogation" as in "interrogation"?' I ask Zoë.

'Rog ... A service for people called Roger?' she suggests.

'"Rogare", Latin for "to ask"?'

Zoë rolls her eyes. 'You and your grammar school.'

'Is it an asking service? Asking for God's forgiveness? Blessing? Help parking? What's an "asking service"?'

'Maybe we should ask someone.'

We're met at the west door by a kind-looking woman with the smile and rosy cheeks of a retired primary school teacher.

'Grab a seat,' she says. 'Don't get comfortable though.'

It's a strangely dismissive welcome, at odds with her warm manner. Our confused look causes her to continue.

'Oh, don't you know?' she says gleefully. 'Today we're beating the bounds.'

* * *

My girlfriend had surprised me with this trip. She told me we were going somewhere in the UK with potentially muddy walks. I knew nothing else, at least till the week before when I needed to go welly-shopping. The shops were lacking – you just can't get a decent boot on the high street nowadays, and Boots don't find it amusing when you ask in there, nor when you storm out bellowing, 'Call yourself a shoe-shop?!'

Outside the shop, I grinned and Zoë cringed, before saying without thinking, 'Don't worry, you'll be able to buy wellies in Devon.'

'In where?'

'In heaven!' she covered. 'You know what they say, "wellies in heaven".'

'That's "pennies from heaven".'

So we came west, me wellyless. It would be a chance to unwind, relax, and step away from the rough and tumble of stage performance. And yet, performer to the last, I can never quite escape it.

'… And no gigging while we're away,' Zoë had said when we'd booked the time off.

'Moi? When would I ever even think of such a thing?'

'Well, we visited your Cornish relatives, but stopped on the way for one gig, you did another in Cornwall, and I had to beg you not to take that "slight diversion" to Birmingham on the way back.'

She had a point. Just as I'm sure Lord Sugar checks his stocks while sunning himself on a yacht, my postman probably sorts the odd bit of mail in Tenerife, and Boris Johnson undoubtedly trips and lands fully-clothed in a swimming pool, so comedians find it difficult to switch off. Whole holidays can be built around where in the country – or the world – we can tell our jokes. The first comedian to Mars will be looking at doing a sneaky gig on Venus before heading home.

This trip would be different. I couldn't promise no performing, but I could promise I'd debut a magic trick I'd been working on.

I'd always liked magic since I was a kid. The problem was I was rubbish at it, a fact especially highlighted when living with old housemate Danny: comedian and magician. Like all good magicians, he'd been doing tricks for as long as he could remember, and he was probably only just born before declaring to the midwife, 'Ba-na!'

My attempts at cups and balls looked a little hopeless next to him plucking cards from nowhere mid-conversation. He'd make whole vases vanish before my eyes. I'd always find them again, and inevitably the back of our sofa had more sponge balls down it than you've ever seen in your life, but what do you expect living with a conjuror? We'd even have his magic pals round for takeaway, and they'd use phrases like 'Zarrow shuffle', 'French drop' and 'Mercury fold' like they were common parlance. I'd try and join in with phrases like 'Marvin's Magic', 'Izzy Wizzy' and 'Got your nose'.

This was my chance to finally add a card trick to my repertoire. I rehearsed every chance I got,[1] bodging it each time, and cursing my uncoordinated fingers. For the first time in a long while I was nervous. Unspeakably nervous.

'Are you all right?' Zoë asked as I drove the first stint of our journey west. 'Do you want me to drive?'

'No,' I insisted, although secretly I did, so I could practise my card-forcing. 'Doing fine. I'll just keep following the satnav to this "mystery destination".'

We arrived in Devon and I faked my astonishment again. I hoped my sleight of hand was going to look more convincing than my surprise-feigning. Still, I had a day or two of holiday yet to work on it.

A genuine and pleasant surprise was the South Hams. It's an untapped gem of England's green and pleasant land, at least untapped as far as I was concerned. If your experience of Devon is either the A-road to get to Cornwall, or taking a right to discover Dartmoor, take a left some time and discover the South Hams: Dartmouth, Salcombe, pubs, beaches and rolling hills – just delightful. Tell them I sent you. Try the fish.

Shortly after arriving we set off to explore and found the neighbouring village of Stoke Fleming, a peaceful settlement that's not only in an Area of Outstanding Natural Beauty, but also is in an area of outstanding natural beauty.[2] Like all proper villages, it had one of everything: one pub, one shop, one school, one seafood restaurant with a fantastically punny name,[3] and one church ...

* * *

'Very special service this morning,' announces the amiable vicar, a middle-aged chap with an accent more Stoke than Stoke Fleming, in shirt, trousers and dog collar rather than full robes. 'Delighted for the good weather which means we can go ahead, and delighted you've all turned out for it.'

Thirty or so locals fill the pews. I presume they're locals. They could

---

[1] I should probably have been packing or buying wellies, but I could always get them in Devon.
[2] Upper case means a panel of bureaucrats think so; lower case means I think so.
[3] The Brill Plaice. What a name.

all be holidaymakers like us, but judging from the smiles we're getting from everyone else, we're the only strangers.

'So today is our Rogation. Are you ready to beat the bounds?'

There's a surprisingly vocal 'Yes!' from the gathered throng, and Zoë and I join in heartily. We're hoping that 'bounds' isn't common parlance for 'newcomers'.

'Then let's go!' the vicar exclaims, and marches down the aisle. Everyone stands and follows. The kindly welcomer gathers us as she exits.

'So you know what "beating the bounds" is?' she asks us.

'I'm afraid not,' says Zoë. We both resist adding, 'We're not from round these parts,' as you can only say so in a mock West Country accent that may be deemed offensive.

'Well today is "Gangday".'

This is getting worse. These parishioners, average age of fifty-five, are going to form a gang, blow off church and beat the bounds out of some poor chap who didn't put enough protection money in the collection coffers last month. They worship rough round here.

'The idea is we're going to beat out the boundary of the village.'

That's a relief.

We exit church with her, after only two minutes inside. It feels like the shortest service we've ever been to. But it's only just begun ...

'In practice we don't beat the whole boundary nowadays on Gangday. We'll drop into a few of the farmers' fields from the village. Chance to ask for the crops to be blessed, and a bit of a nose round, see who's having what extensions done ...' She remembers herself. 'Times were, they'd go round the parish boundary and pray for God's protection on everything inside it.'

On second thoughts, it does sound a bit gang-ish. It's the middle England equivalent of tribalism: standing on the edge of your parish line, asking for divine blessing for one side of it, and not for the other.

The welcomer introduces herself as Shirley, and explains more as we walk to our first stop on our village tour. Evidently this is an optional service for parishes, but some country churches like this one still like to do it. Before maps were commonplace, beating the boundary with a birch bough was a way of passing down the knowledge of parish boundaries. It was important for at least some people in each parish to know where the borders were, to show who could marry where, and ultimately who could be buried where. These boundaries still matter today, when it comes to permitting weddings in particular churches, only today you can search online and find out in a Google-boasting 0.22 seconds which parish is yours. Pre-maps, you'd have to locate the right church officials who'd know, or find the parish boundary stones, both taking an unknown amount of time, since they happened pre-stopwatch.

One key feature of the day was that the old and the young were part of the village perambulation, so that the geographical knowledge could be passed down the generations. Traditionally the boys brought along would be whipped, or even bumped violently on the boundary stones, to help them remember exactly where the parish line was. They'd then be given money, to help them forget.[4] It seems that while the practical point was to ensure everyone knew where the boundaries were, there were no such boundaries when it came to church officials beating children.

It's appropriate then that we decided to attend this service, since we are by some way the youngest here, apart from two ten-year-olds. We, and I'm sure the ten-year-olds, are hoping the stone-bumping is in the past. There's every chance that some of the eighty-year-olds remember what it was like.

We're on board with it, despite my uncertainties that this may yet end up somewhere between *Children of the Corn* and *The Wicker Man*. Zoë has thankfully seen neither film, otherwise she'd be clambering back over that handbrake before you could say 'Wellies in Devon'. Instead we arrive at our first field.

The vicar slowly opens the gate, shouting, 'We're coming in!' as if he's a hostage negotiator. We all know he's just fearful of a farmer with a big shotgun. Nothing puts a dampener on a Rogation Sunday more than a shot vicar.

The farmer appears from across the field and joins us for this stint. He doesn't strike me as a churchgoing man – his arms are firmly folded and he looks a little baffled by thirty Christians occupying his land when they should be in church. But he's also one to hedge his bets, while we bet on his hedges. If we can encourage God's blessing on his crops, he'll take it.

Prayers are said for his crops, and those of other farmers in the parish. He's grateful we've stopped by, although is perhaps a little unsettled when

---

[4] Forget the pain, not the new boundary knowledge.

one parishioner starts strumming a guitar, and we all stay for a hymn. We're all given a hymn sheet.[5] This service is truly retro, showing life pre-projectors, pre-maps, and for some chilly congregants, pre-coats.

The worship leader starts up with 'All Creatures of our God and King', which makes me scour the landscape for signs of animals. If he's an arable farmer, he'll be a bit less bothered about the 'creatures' of the title than if it's a pastoral farm. In fact if he just grows crops, the 'creatures' we're singing about will probably do more damage than good. I spy a sheep, and carry on singing.

* * *

In the chalet kitchenette, I was finishing my morning's magic practice; I was pretty smooth with it, I thought as I picked up the rogue cards that had rudely fallen to the floor mid-flourish. Later that day, I'd be performing this trick for real for the first – and probably last – time.

'What are you doing with the cards?' Zoë said, somehow before she was even in the room.

'Just practising a trick,' I replied nervously. 'I'll show it to you … in a bit.'

'Yeah, you want to get it right. I remember when you tried to produce that coin from my ear. Could have done with more practice there.'

'Sorry again about that earring. Does it still hurt?'

'It's healing.'

I bottled my nerves about the later event, and tried to focus on enjoying our break. It was like the background image of my brain had a nice holiday vista, but the foreground had the word 'Panic!' flashing in big letters. I tried to distract myself with our spoils from Tourist Information.

'Soooooo, a Saturday in Devon. What do you fancy?' I asked, flicking through the leaflets. 'We've got National Trust, English Heritage and a What's On In Suffolk pamphlet that must have been put in the wrong stand.'

'Let's find somewhere picturesque,' she suggested. 'What about Dartmoor?'

It's a barren landscape with a prison in the middle, but it sounded

---

[5] Remember hymn sheets? They were before we had projected words on screens.

good to me. Besides it was nearer than Suffolk. I grabbed my deck of cards and other essentials for later, and we headed north. North Devon, but that's still north.

As we drove, anxiety stole my speech. I was just beginning to worry that if I didn't speak soon, then Zoë would start talking about something serious, when she broke the silence:

'I wonder, can I just ask, have you thought about, you know, where we're going?'

Oh no. I'd missed the small talk window. We could have been having a meaningless conversation about which Devon village name sounds most like a Victorian sleuth,[6] or a completely different conversation about which Devon village name sounds most like a clothing shop for monarchs.[7] Instead we'd ended up talking about Big Stuff. Inevitably on or after trips away with other halves, relationships shift and this topic comes up, but not here, not now.

'Because we could always pull over and get the map out of the boot,' Zoë continued.

Such relief. She was only doubting my geographical skills. Partly to reassert my directional ability, and partly to ensure the conversation stayed meaningless, I told her we didn't need the map and suggested we spot place names that sound like Victorian sleuths.

We passed a sign to Chudleigh Knighton, and chuckled.

* * *

I feel like a Christian Hare Krishna. We're getting looks as we stride down the main street of Stoke Fleming, singing 'We Are Marching' and looking in the hedgerow for the elusive gap to a farmer's footpath. A caravanning couple chortle as they see us. Some early Sunday lunchers look up from their pints at a pub picnic table. I want to explain that we're beating the bounds, and that if it weren't for us doing this, they wouldn't know where they could be buried.

The Rogation service has lost its practical necessity today of course – we've got maps, whether in the boot or elsewhere. Walking around, we haven't even got a birch bough to do any beating, and so far none of the younger generation have been bounced on a boundary

---

[6] Surely Berry Pomeroy or Aveton Gifford.
[7] It's Kingswear.

stone by any of the older folks. In fact I'd wager that our bottoms are less sore than at most pew-based Sunday services.

We come to rest in a woodland, and Psalm 104 is read – a favourite at such services, our welcomer tells us.

'Only one more stop,' says Shirley as the reading finishes. 'Bet you're wishing you brought wellies.' Her eyes are drawn down to my muddy trainers, and Zoë's smug, snug boots.

I frown and Shirley continues, 'These walks used to take days when they did the whole border. Mostly because they had to find all the boundary stones and people kept moving them. You know, landowners trying to cheat it.'

Shirley points to a tall moustachioed man with an air of *Downton Abbey* to him. 'We're off to his garden next. Well it's more of an estate.' I make a mental note to not be left with him and one space in a lifeboat. We've all seen *Titanic*.

Apparently they used to beat the bounds through properties without permission if need be. If your house had the misfortune to straddle the parish line, you'd need to expect the vicar and his twig-bearing parishioners at any time, not to mention local urchins holding a few pence and their behinds.

The thirty of us have now become twenty or so – a few infirm folks have dropped out and a couple of others have gone back to open the church and brew the tea. The rest of us walk to our last stop, and Shirley uses the chance to ask about us.

'So you're down for a holiday?'

'Yes,' Zoë replies. 'It's been, er ... eventful.'

'Oh?' Shirley enquires. She's evidently the parish gossip.

So we tell her about Dartmoor.

*   *   *

Brown signs were everywhere, offering pubs, museums and stone circles. None were hitting the mark for us, although Castle Drogo sounded nicely archaic. It was clearly full of cauldrons and goblins, not to mention evil Count Drogo who spent his days on the turret walls maniacally laughing.

It was a bit far though, so we opted for 'Canonteign Falls: England's highest waterfall'. Zoë liked a waterfall and I liked anything record-breaking, so in we popped. The views at the top were apparently breathtaking, although that could be a result of the steep climb.

We parked, and I strode up at a surprisingly quick pace, given my general suspicion of exercise.

'Is there a rush?' Zoë panted. 'I've never seen you walk so fast. We're here all day. Unless you wanted to try and also make ... Castle Drogo!' She gave a maniacal laugh. Scared, I strode on twice as fast.

'It's your wellies – they're slowing you down!' I shouted back to her, as I marched straight into a puddle.

We reached the top, to find a stunning view of edge-of-Dartmoor farmland, and a collection of annoying tourists.

After a minute, Zoë headed for the clamber down. 'Well, that was nice.'

'Hold on,' I said. 'The others are going in a second. Imagine the view without them in front of it.'

They continued to take each other's photos standing in front of every inch of the landscape while playing the hilarious game of 'back a bit, back a bit more'.

'No they're not,' Zoë said.

'Well, they will in a minute.'

Ten minutes later they left, and the view was finally ours. It was nice.

'Do you want to see that magic trick?' I asked from nowhere. I equally tried producing the pack of cards from nowhere, but nearly lost them down the waterfall.

'What? Here? Why on earth have you brought those with you?'

'Yeah, well we've seen the view now. So do you want to see my card trick?'

I'm guessing it was the first and only magic trick to be attempted atop England's highest waterfall, at least until David Blaine scrapes the barrel of ideas with his TV spectacular 'CanonBlaine Falls', which coincidentally would feature him literally scraping a barrel.

'Well... all right then,' she sighed. 'Since you've brought the cards all the way to the top of a waterfall. Ever the performer, even on holiday ...'.

She was a bit confused, which was the general idea. I asked her to pick a card, any card, then pick another card, any other card.

'Right, now you've got two cards memorised, and I haven't seen either, yes?'

'Yes, apparently.'

'Okay, now for each card, just think of it as a number and a suit, so

Three of Clubs is "Three Clubs", okay? And Ace is One, Jack is Eleven, Queen's Twelve, King's Thirteen.'

'O … kay,' she said hesitantly.

'Right. Close your eyes.'

'Don't push me off.'

I promised not to, and she closed her eyes. I knelt, and took out the other item in my pocket.

'Now tell me what cards you've got.'

'Out loud?'

'Yes, out loud.'

'Umm …'

Please say you've remembered them.

'Two of Hearts, Ace of …'

'As a number, and without the 'of'.' My knee was on stone, and my balance was going.

'Oh, Two Hearts and … Ace is Eleven?'

'One, Ace is One.'

'Two Diamonds …'

'Hearts. You said it was Hearts.'

'It was a while ago, I've forgotten. No wait, it's … Two Hearts, One Diamond.'

'Open your eyes.'

She opened her eyes, looked ahead for a split-second and didn't see me, then to the ground, where I was nearly toppling over the edge of the waterfall, with a diamond ring in its open case.

I used her full name – something only ever done when telling someone off or proposing – and asked her to marry me.

* * *

'What did she say?!' Shirley exclaims.

I'm surprised she has to ask, since Zoë's right here. Either it was a yes or a very gentle turn-down.

It's clear we have Shirley's full attention – she's ignored several house extensions that others are peering at. Some have sidled over to us though to listen. One woman speaks up.

'Well?'

* * *

After a good minute of delight, cheer and general amazement at my card-forcing skills, we realised that Zoë hadn't given me an answer.

'Oh, and yes, by the way!' she added with a grin.

I replaced the cards in my pocket – their purpose was done and wouldn't be needed again, unless we were going to draw a high card to see who gets first choice of honeymoon. There were no gigs this holiday thankfully, which was a good job as I couldn't handle any more nerves.

Another group of tourists timed it perfectly and arrived just as we left the crest of the waterfall. Any earlier and they'd have witnessed the lot. The last thing I wanted during the proposal was a holidaying family pointing and yelling, 'That's not a free choice! He's moved the Ace from the front of the pack!'

And we climbed down Canonteign: the English couple who went up a hill, and came down engaged.

* * *

'Oh, how lovely!' Shirley shakes both our hands, and her and other listeners smile at us throughout the short sermon that follows in the garden.

One of the eavesdroppers, a gaunt elderly lady with a glint in her eye, sidles up to me and mimes a fanned pack of cards. 'Lucky she didn't pick the Joker,' she says with a nudge.

In many ways she did.

After a short walk back into church, we take our original seats and the vicar makes his way to the front.

'A lovely walk. A lovely Rogation. And a lovely hymn now to close. Before we sing though, I've just been told by Shirley that she's been talking to our young friends who've joined us, Paul and Zoë ...'

I gulp. We're about to be told off for chatting en route.

'... who both got engaged yesterday. Isn't that nice?!'

Phew.

The congregation give a little applause, and the vicar leads a kind prayer for us. We're very humbled by their warm welcome and good wishes.

The closing song finishes and we stay for coffee. Many of the congregants come to wish us well, and one of them, a kind-faced octogenarian, gives us a little tour of the church's architectural features. He shows us with pride the eighteenth-century font, the stained glass windows and the solid wood pulpit, designed and created by a local schoolgirl a century ago. She was fourteen when she carved it. Perhaps it even excused her from being bumped on the stones that May.

For my fiancée and I, the whole experience has been the perfect start to our journey towards marriage. The worshippers came to ask a divine blessing on the crops: that they grow, that the seasons are kind to them, that they will weather storms and sustain life. And we've done likewise.

8

Doubled Up

Believing with Baptists

'This is a big roundabout,' said Rob, designated driver for our trip from London to the North West.

'What, you mean Birmingham?' I asked.

'Yeah.'

'Is that why you've been indicating for three miles?'

'Oh.'

Rob stopped signalling, a good ten miles before turning off for the M6.

I'd cut short the day's wedding planning – now on month three and still umming and ahhing about menu options – for the long trip to a Baptist church in the North West. Rob and I were to put on a couple of hours of comedy at an event we were told was aiming for 5% church folks/95% local community. We were pretty convinced it would be almost the exact opposite.

Rob offered me a Starburst on the condition that I called it an Opal Fruit, and asked: 'Are you doing your Adam and Eve jokes? Cos if you are, I won't do mine.'

He was not a churchgoer, but had written a few Bible jokes in readiness for the gig, ever since I booked him for it a few months back.

'It's fine,' I said, chewing a Starburst. 'If you do them, I'll drop mine. Or I'll just do them anyway and say it's a callback.'

The over-repetition of jokes was on my mind. What happens if you hear a joke too many times? And more importantly, what happens if you hear a joke too many times?

As well as being a stand-up comic I'm also a sit-down writer, mainly suggesting additional material on various sitcom scripts. As a stand-up, you can repeat gags each night to different audiences, for a while, till the idea of repeating the same old rubbish fills you with dread and you're forced to write something new. As a script writer, every line must be fresh. TV consumes gags faster than Rob consumes Starbursts.[1]

'So you busy as a writer then?' Rob asked, as we faced off against three lanes of brake lights.

I had been, and a little too busy if honest. A few months back I'd been working across two shows at once, punching up Show A at home or on the commute to Show B, which had a writer's room. Half a dozen of us would sit around a desk of coffee and doughnuts from nine till five. Then I'd be back on the train working on Show A again. I'd work on one show alone, and the other with others – a perfect mix.

You can 'double up' as a stand-up quite easily – opening at one venue and closing at another. However there can be stand-up double-up hiccups. You can tell a joke at Venue B that you thought you'd only done at Venue A, but you might have also done at Venue B just five minutes earlier. Although rarer, something similar can happen as a writer.

Weeks after working on Shows A and B, a draft of an episode of Show A arrived for me to punch up. My eyes were drawn to a gag that I recognised, not from this show but from the other. A knot formed in my stomach. It was here in this show, yet I was convinced that I'd submitted it for the other. Either my mind was playing tricks on me, or I was in trouble.

I chased back through my emails in a panic, muttering 'No, no, no, no ...', and sure enough there it was. Alt-tabbing on the computer, I could see the same line, written by me, in scripts for two completely different sitcoms: Show A, a post-watershed flatshare sitcom, and Show B, a pre-watershed family sitcom.

'So what you writing on at the moment?' Rob asked, as we finally joined the M6.

'This and that,' I replied. I told him about 'this' and I told him about 'that', and how the same joke featured in both.

The shows had names, but I won't mention them here, to minimise trouble. I did give the names to Rob.

'Not heard of them,' came his honest answer. 'And you didn't realise at the time?'

'Honestly, no. I wrote it for the first show, and just sent it off into the joke mill.' You always hope it'll be kneaded into comic goodness, but

---

[1] They're not Opal Fruits, and he's lying to himself.

you know that more likely they'll just dispose of it as industrial waste. 'Weeks later I pitched it again to a roomful of writers. My brain never told me I'd already sold it to someone else.'

It was so rare that a gag could be used in two different shows. Sitcoms aren't just a collection of random jokes, and most lines in a script are going to be so tightly relevant to the show that you can't conceive of it working elsewhere. A line from Del Boy wouldn't sound right coming out of Joey Tribbiani's mouth. Yet in this instance, Shows A and B had somehow ended up with similar plotlines, both vaguely involving small children, football and hospitalisation. It was the perfect storm. It meant that what we'll call 'Gag Zero' could have found a home in either show, and unfortunately it was now squatting in both.

'I wouldn't worry,' Rob tried to placate me. 'So what if they are the same? I'm sure I heard a line from *The Office* on some American sitcom recently. What was it now ... ?'

I sensed his joke. 'Was it the American version of *The Office*?'

'Yeah, something like that,' he replied with a laugh, and retuned the radio to Radio 1. I knew on his own he was a Capital Gold man, but he had a car-sharer to impress.

Rob turned up the dance track playing and shouted over it. 'My point is, you're not going to get the same audience for both shows. Even if it makes the cut, twice, they'll be broadcast far apart, different channels ...'

'No, same channel.'

'Is it E4? No one watches E4. I was in a pilot on E4. No one watched it. I couldn't believe it.'

'When was that on?'

'I don't know. I didn't watch it.'

'Well one's on tonight, 8.30, BBC1. And the other one by contrast is on tonight, 9.30, BBC1.'

'Ah,' Rob concluded. 'You're in trouble.'

This was why it had been laying in my stomach for weeks like a bad vindaloo. There was nothing I could do about it. Not at this late stage.

'You worried?' he asked.

'I've been bricking it for weeks. I should have said something. Instead I've been tearing my hair out at home. We've been trying to plan a wedding and I've not been able to focus on it.'

Radio 1 cut to the news and Rob turned it off. After a minute's quiet, he asked: 'Hey, what was the joke?'

I'm not going to tell it here, in print. I've no idea of the repercussions of even mentioning that this happened. By the time you read this, I could be locked up in the tower.

When I first found out about my mistake, I merely predicted a stern talking to. As I spoke to Rob, several hours before my gag could be broadcast to the nation, twice, I was predicting government-led inquiries and an overhaul of the licence fee. I won't add to the risk of a major Newsnight investigation by being too specific here.

I told Rob the joke and silence filled the car. For the first time, I wished Radio 1 was still on so I could at least kid myself that the phat beats were hiding his laughter.

'Don't worry, they won't use that,' he said seriously.

He was right. It wasn't exactly a world-beater. The joke's quality alone would probably see it edited out, plus each script had numerous hurdles before it hit the screens. All I knew though was that when I last saw both scripts, Gag Zero was still staring out at me, like your mate in a shop window display doing a silly dance. You know you have to get him out of there before too many people see, but you have no idea how.

We parked at the Baptist church beneath a banner declaring 'Comedy Night!', and Rob and I both stretched as we left the car from the long drive.

Rob yawned. 'Well, if no one shows up, we can go and watch TV somewhere, see if your jokes made it. Although it does mean hearing that joke again. Twice.'

We opened the centre doors to find an eager audience awaiting us. TV would wait. At least with this lot here, there'd be a couple of hundred less witnesses to the televisual mayhem.

Rob nudged me and whispered, 'Here, what if a royal dies? Then they'll cancel all the telly.'

'Ssh, Rob. We're in a church.'

A fifty-year-old man jogged over to us and said, 'Welcome! Now remember, you're not in a church ... '

I was confused. I thought we were in a church.

'Ah, no, no, well, we are in a "church", but we're not in a "church". I'm Pete the pastor, by the way.'

I looked around, and Pastor Pete had a point. The venue was full of audience, with stage and lights and sound-desk, but no cross, no altar, and no paraphernalia. No banners from the Mothers' Union, no church organ and no collection of instruments in the corner.

'We do film nights, fish and chip suppers, and now we thought we'd have you guys.' He nodded to some twenty-somethings giggling in the corner. 'They want poker nights. I tell them to dream on.'

Rob was looking around just as I was, trying to get the measure of the place. 'So is this a Baptist church ... centre ... thing?'

'Yeah, on a Sunday,' Pete replied. 'Tonight it's just another venue.'

Rob looked crestfallen. 'But I've written some Bible jokes. I've even read up on Baptists ... '

John, the other Baptist

John Smyth was an English priest who left the Church of England and led a small congregation in Holland. In 1609, he stood atop one of Holland's highest points, a good three centimetres off the ground, and read all the Bible verses that refer to infant baptism:

'   ,

'   ,

and most importantly

'   ,

There aren't any, and that was the basis of the Baptist movement. Apart from that, they are autonomous and so very different. They can do what they like, and convert their church building into a comedy night, without so much as a form to fill in. Just don't fall in the pool ...

'Have you got sharks?' asked Rob.

Pete gave a chuckle. 'That's Bond villains! You watch out. You'll be standing right over the pool, and I've got the button right here.'

Rob looked genuinely fearful.

I tried to put my sitcom-writing worries to one side, but it was still gnawing away at me. This, and showtime due any minute, sent me to the Gents.

There I found various posters of community info – you could read about a film night or an art sale while washing your hands. In the cubicles, they'd hidden the faith-based posters. Behind my toilet door was an A4 poster giving a modern approach to prayer. It read, 'If you know someone in need of it, use your phone to take a photo of this prayer, and text it to them'. Then followed three lines of hope, thanksgiving and general niceness, plus a note about washing your hands that probably wasn't part of the prayer.

I liked it. It was a neat technological twist, even if it was found in an unusual place, but I suppose they had got a captive audience here in the cubicle. It certainly worked for me anyway, and I obeyed its instructions. My wife-to-be had put up with my anxious nonsense for weeks, ever since Gag-gate. She deserved to know I was thinking about her, and if I took the photo close enough she'd never know this was actually a toilet.

I lined it up and clicked, and my phone gave its old-fashioned camera-noise.

Emerging from the cubicle, I saw Pastor Pete washing his hands. His calm and jokey demeanour from earlier had faded a little, and he looked alarmed.

'What were you doing in there?' he enquired, gesturing to the cubicle. 'What was that noise?'

'Oh, that. It's the camera on my phone. Does it when I take a photo.' And I thought this was meant to be a modern church.

I washed and dried my hands under the posters, deciding, if I were local, which art print I'd buy, and whether I'd watch *Chicken Run* on Saturday at 3.30 p.m. with popcorn or Twiglets. Zoë would choose popcorn. Rob would have Opal Fruits, although I don't know how he managed to join our hypothetical house-share.

I started to message Zoë the prayer-photo as I left the Gents.

'What are you doing now?' Pastor Pete continued.

'Oh, I'm just texting the photo.'

'What, from the cubicle?' he asked.

'Yes, I'm sending it to my fiancée. I want to say sorry for being a misery guts. Thought it'd be nice.'

And I left the loos, and Pastor Pete's worried expression.

I found Rob pacing the floor near the auditorium, ready to take the stage.

'You good?' I asked him.

'Yeah. You?'

'Mmm. Nervous.'

'About the gig or your jokes on telly? Half eight now. Your first show's on.'

The gig wasn't occupying my mind at all. I told Rob he had been right on the drive up – I should have told someone about the doubling up. Now it was too late.

'Might ease your conscience if you just tell someone. Can you confess to Pete? He's a priest.'

'He's a pastor. They don't do confession via church leaders here.'

'Well just tell him anyway. Might help you have a good gig.'

Rob talked sense. I decided I needed to get my writing woes off my chest to someone other than a Starburst-chewing Capital Gold fan, so I sought out Pete, who still looked gravely concerned about something.

'Pete,' I said. 'I hope you don't mind. I know it's not a confessional moment or anything, but I just wanted to run something past you. I don't think it's a 'sin', as such. But I messed up. See, I sent something I really shouldn't have sent ...'

'Oh I know you did!' Pete said accusingly.

'... It's only a joke, but ...'

'Didn't look like a joke to me!'

Eh? Had Rob explained? Had Pastor Pete nipped to a side room and watched my joke on TV?

'Oh you've seen it? What did you think of it?'

'No I haven't seen it and what you do in there ...'

He pointed to the Gents. Ohhhhhhh ...

'No! Not in there ...You know about the prayer poster in the toilets? I wasn't ... No! I wasn't texting anything else ...'

'Your fiancée? Look, this is my church!'

I thought this wasn't a church, but it wasn't the time to correct him.

After *a lot* of explaining about prayer posters and camera phones and sitcom-writing, Pastor Pete and I made up, and Rob and I had a fine evening with the two hundred comedygoers – which were indeed 95% locals.

On the drive home I resolved to do several things:

- Confess to producers of both shows what happened, regardless of whether the line is doubled up or not.
- Be extra vigilant in future to make sure this doesn't happen again.
- Buy more Starburst.

Once home, I couldn't wait any longer. I watched a recording of the pre-watershed family sitcom first. Ten minutes in, there it was: Gag Zero. Oh no, no, no! Broadcast at the same time as I was floundering to a Baptist minister. I didn't even watch the rest of the episode; I skipped straight to the 9.30 p.m. show to see if Gag Zero made a second unwelcome appearance.

I knew it belonged in the first five minutes, and when the scene it belonged in didn't appear, I high-fived myself. They cut it out! I would live! Admittedly they might have cut it out because some editor-in-chief spotted Gag Zero at zero hour, in which case I might still be for the high jump, but for now I was jumping for joy.

I texted Zoë the good news. She replied instantly saying she was delighted, and thanks for the prayer message asking her to please wash her hands. She'd be more than happy to wash her hands of my doubling up worries, and could we now get back to this wedding table-plan.

Later that week, I spoke to the producer of the other sitcom nonchalantly in passing, for no reason or anything, just saying hi, and by the way were there many last-minute cuts in that episode?

Yes, he said. That scene involving the football, the children and the kitchen implement sadly had to go, just because of time, and the plot made equal sense without it. Sorry, he said.

'Oh no need to apologise ...' I replied. And that would have been the perfect time to make good on my wish to confess all.

I did not make good on that. I'm not meant to confess to a Baptist minister, and I couldn't bring myself to confess to the producers. So I'm going to confess here. Well I mean I have. I'm not now going to write the chapter out again. That would be doubling up.

9

Lost at Sea

iCebergs and iChurch

So we wedded. I often doubted I'd ever marry, thinking weddings for me were like planes – I'm more often pressed up against the window than anywhere near the aisle. But the big day was excellent and the bride looked amazing. We danced down the aisle as husband and wife, and onto a fine reception where wine was drunk and relatives were drunk.

I learnt that being both groom and comedian was a tricky balance to manage. I had to be quite clear in my head that, pre-wedding, no jokes were allowed. Nothing about the wedding was funny. I found out to my cost that it's bad form to suggest 'I Still Haven't Found What I'm Looking For' as a first dance.

Oh, and don't go telling your wife-to-be the night before that you've got *Cold Feet*, before presenting her with a DVD of the same name. It's. Never. Funny.

Soon after my own wedding, I was asked to play a gig at someone else's. They're not easy gigs, which surprises some people. 'But everyone's in a good mood,' you might say. 'Laughter will surely flow like water off England's highest waterfall.'

In theory yes, but inevitably the comedian is squeezed in between the speeches and the disco. The assembled mass have already laughed and just want a boogie. Plus everyone wants to know who are you and why you have infiltrated their get-together.

Some days when the call comes in though, you forget all this. Besides, the happy couple were friends of friends, so what could possibly go wrong? Let's find out ...

The wedding was at Britain's only surfers' church, called Tubestation. Despite its name it was a long way from the London Underground, based in Polzeath on Cornwall's north coast. The idea appealed: a church aimed at a very specific group of people, there for its community as well as visiting holidaymakers.

They'd had a great ceremony, a grand meal and uproarious speeches, which meant it was time for me to come along and ride that wave of good will. I followed the first dance – a tall order. No wonder those Abba-esque dancefloors can look a bit bleak after the first dance. How do you follow that? With thirty minutes of a ginger man talking, that's how.

Bless them, the bride and groom and a few others stuck around for my attempt to follow one of the most magical moments of their lives. There were no chairs, as I was performing to the dancefloor. I went down like ... well, like a stranger at a wedding. The buffet was being served as I started, so a good deal of my potential audience quite rightly ran off towards that. I know that if I was faced with the option of standing listening to me, or eating a plate of goujons, it would be breaded chicken every time.

The new Mr and Mrs were magnificent hosts, and like a great comedian once told me of wedding gigs, 'You have a bad show in a club, you get over it at the next gig. You have a bad gig at a wedding, you'll always be the guy who ruined their big day.'

So if they ever read this, I hope I wasn't the guy who ruined your big day. I'm hoping that was some other guy, or even better, that your day wasn't ruined.

Danger! Tough gig ahead
Warning signs to watch out for:

Is something else on offer mid-performance?
A lot of performances rise and fall based around what else is on offer, whether it's a buffet, the bar being open, or a naked man out of the window. All of these have happened while I've been onstage.

The naked man was at a student gig in Newcastle where large windows flanked the venue. Mid-performance, a wandering eye in the audience noticed the fellow, clotheless and clueless in his dorm room kitchen. He overlooked the students' union, and was

---

also overlooking basic health and safety by cooking bacon with not a stitch on. Pretty soon we had to stop the gig mid-joke, as the entire audience could not resist a peek. The fascination was not so much with the fact that he was naked, but the scary uncertainty of what would happen when the fat reached a high temperature and started to spatter. The audience cries of, 'Get some curtains!' were replaced by, 'Get an apron!' as we began to understand the ticking time bomb of bacon grease.

After two electrifying minutes, we visibly saw the fat jump out of the pan, followed by Student Naked Guy jumping back with a horribly pained expression on his face.[1] We heard his yelp, he heard ours, he screamed back at us, reached for a curtain that wasn't there, which gave us all an even clearer view of his mixed grill, then leapt back to turn off the light. The kitchen was plunged into darkness, and the audience groaned at the loss of their entertainment. I reluctantly returned to the stage to try and follow that little show, as we heard the clatter of dropping pans in the pitch-black kitchen over the path, and more yelping.

Is someone better performing within earshot?

Mid-joke in a tent at Guildford's 'GuilFest' festival, I heard the muffled announcement across the site: '... Please welcome to the stage, Rolf Harris!' The large audience upped and left quicker than you could say 'didgeridoo', let alone anything about the ladies of the harem of the court of King Caractacus. Five minutes later it started raining and new punters, who were just passing by, ran in for cover. That's when you realise that sometimes your show is nothing more than a big umbrella, or a waiting room for a bigger act on a few stages down.

Is there a dress code?

If you're told by the person booking you that you simply *have to* wear a suit for the show, then that's a very strong indication that

---

[1] This is a guess. No one was looking at his face.

laughs may be trickier to come by. Weddings, corporate gigs, funerals – all can go marvellously, but all have a much higher death-rate, especially the funerals.

I don't mean gigs where suits are optional. I've worn many a two-piece[2] at regular comedy clubs. No, it's when you are absolutely required to dig out your Tesco Value jacket and trouser set. That's when to start sweating, and not just because it's too tight and made of 100% polyester.

At one such event I endured a forty-minute sponsored silence to a group of masons. 'Pull out the bankers,' I thought to myself, meaning 'do my best jokes' but also 'those chatty bankers at the table near the back – someone pull them out'. Which brings me to ...

Is the entire audience made up of wealthy, elderly, white males?...

In my experience, this is the hardest group of people to make laugh, which is a shame because one day I was really hoping to become one. The odds of me ending my days as a young, poor, black woman are highly unlikely – a pity, as I'd at least laugh now and then.

The wealthier the audience, the less laughter you can hope to get from them, perhaps because they're happy enough in their lives. This theory was explored at a strange gig in Monaco. We were instructed before taking to the stage at the noted tax haven not to ask what anyone does for a living ... which is a red rag to a bull. Asking a comedian not to mention something onstage is like saying don't think of a purple elephant: you simply have to, especially when faced with an audience who could have a red rag, a bull and a purple elephant airlifted here within the hour, just because they felt like it.

Thankfully I was the closing act that night, so by the time I went onstage, all the awkward questions had been asked ... 'What do you do for a living?' 'Which yacht in the harbour is yours?'

[2] Not that sort of two-piece.

'Only a twelve-berth, three-storey yacht? Could you not have tried a little bit harder in school?'

Each question, like their tax, was mostly avoided. The laughs, like the ages of the billionaires and their female partners, had very large gaps.

Soon after our wedding, another odd gig was on the horizon – my first cruise.

I relished the opportunity: I'd get to do a one-man show and I always fancied myself as a man of the sea. Plus, as long as the act was the only thing going down terribly and not the ship, it could never be that bad. I knew too that the cruise ship pros were flown all around the world: Panama, Siberia and Great Yarmouth awaited me.

My cruise was to depart from Southampton and dock in Lisbon, from where I'd be flown home. The ship would then sail on to the Canary Islands, and some lucky comedian would take over from me. I'd get the rocky Bay of Biscay, and he'd get the sun-kissed islands, but hey, a cruise is a cruise.

The night before setting sail, or rrmmming the motors, or whatever they call it on big ships, I had a standard circuit gig in Nottingham. Post-show, as is customary when I'm in the locale, I swung by Tipoo Kebab House on Alfreton Road for the best kebab I've yet found on these shores. Since I was a student in Nottingham, the doner in naan bread, all the salad, mild chilli sauce, a dash of lemon and a splat of mint sauce, has been my takeaway of choice.

I knew the Tipoo guys well, and we even exchanged Christmas cards. Multi-faith dialogue in action, if ever I saw it, with a Muslim and a Christian exchanging greetings of a Christian festival while eating halal meat.

Sadly on this occasion, there was to be no Christmas card, and not just because it was summer; they were closed for refurbishment. I was loyal but hungry, so I took my slavering elsewhere and indulged in a sub-par doner wrap (No mint sauce? A scandal) from a roadside van. I ate, felt bad about my betrayal, felt bad because I'd eaten a dodgy kebab, then headed home to sleep before braving the ocean.

On the morning of the cruise my wife bade me goodbye, waving me off with a handkerchief. Well, she actually threw it at me, with the bidding, 'Chilli sauce on your shirt.'

I arrived at the behemoth of a ship with a bad gut feeling, and not just because I was carrying a suit bag and therefore the 'Tough Gig Rule' was in play. My kebab weighed heavily on me. This must be what it feels like to smuggle drugs, I thought as I lolled over to the check-in desk, hoping my passport photo would resemble the green face I sported today.

Anti-norovirus signs warned that any passenger with a gurgling stomach should turn back now. These good people had not spent thousands of pounds – or a tenner on Groupon – to have their head down a toilet for the next eleven days, so all dodgy tummies were to be left in Blighty.

Should I declare it? I decided not to. I knew the origins of my ill-feeling, and this was no infectious sickness virus – just a kebab van lacking a mild version of their chilli, or anywhere to wash their hands. They're off my Christmas card list. So I boarded and lay low. A short rest would solve my tummy-based problems.

I felt no change till an hour later, when I suddenly felt a heck of a lot worse. By chance it was when we left Southampton docks with a jolt. I was surprised. This ship was huge – nineteen floors, several thousand rooms, a casino, a cinema, a shopping mall. Boats rocked. Floating metropolises surely don't rock.

It turns out they do, and so we lurched right to left, or port to starboard, or mint side of tummy to lemon side of tummy, for the next four days, with no let-up and no recovery for my poor tum. The kebab was not a bad idea. The cruise was not a bad idea. The combination was a bad idea.

Thankfully my one and only performance wasn't for a good day and a half, so when entertainment director Vinod introduced me to all the ship's distractions, I told him that I would enjoy them the following night. In truth, I barely left my cabin. For thirty-six hours, I slept, or tried to.

Bad nightmare gave way to bad daydream, all of them taking place on rocking things. I dreamt of the magic carpet ride at Thorpe Park, and of crossing a dodgily swaying suspension bridge. I even had the familiar running-in-treacle frustration dream, only this time I was in a boat on the treacle, and again we just rocked.

In my times of waking, I'd try the ol' 'Keep your eyes on the horizon' trick, but my porthole view just made things worse. Flotsam and jetsam raced past the window. There was not so much as a seagull to distract from the rolling water, which just looked like a magnified version of what was in my stomach. I should have declared at check-in, I thought. Or not had the kebab, but I can never regret a kebab, donerphile that I am. If the afterlife is individually designed with handpicked delights, my heaven will be a kebabylon.

My cabin phone rang with a reminder of my call-time, and as I donned my suit and my show time face, I peered at my reflection in the tiny cabin mirror. The suit was a good fit, but the show time face wasn't. Staring back at me was a shell of a man – not Mr Saturday Night but Mr Still Getting Over Thursday Night.

The commute from my cabin to the theatre was surprisingly long. This ship was big. It took a solid fifteen minutes, without even allowing for me steadying myself against walls. None of the couples I passed were joining me in clinging to the swaying ship. All were sixty-plus, and most were eighty-plus. Yet the spritely thirty-something was the one acting like he was in the latter half of *The Poseidon Adventure*, while they glided with the grace of the toffs from the first half of *Titanic*, or even any non-nautical standard film where people just walked. I heard one couple talk of this as their fifteenth cruise – I imagined you got used to the swaying feeling after that many trips, let alone, guessing their age, the time possibly spent at Dunkirk or Trafalgar.

For the first time I realised that this was my potential audience, and it was a much higher average age than I was used to. Jokes are jokes of course, but I thought I may have to drop some of the gags about Facebook, Duran Duran and the post-Armada era. I convinced myself that other younger passengers would fill the audience too, when a mobility scooter ran over my feet.

Without so much as an apology or an exchange of insurance details, the scooter was off into the distance. That struck me as a great way to get around this ship. Forget the fifteen-minute commute – I needed a shuttle service. The next mobility scooter I saw, I'd hitch a lift.

Unfortunately none came, so I arrived at the theatre tired, with run-over feet and a reeling stomach.

'You enjoy the buffet?' asked entertainment director Vinod from the stage.

'Mmm!' I shouted from forty rows back, the thought of it making me gag.

After a quick mic test, the doors were opened. The couple on their fifteenth cruise made a beeline for the back row, and three mobility scooters entered from different doors and narrowly avoided a collision.

'They're not exactly flooding in,' I said to Vinod backstage. 'More of a trickle.'

'We don't use those words at sea,' Vinod warned. He had a point. I made a mental note not to say later that I'd 'stormed' it, nor that I'd 'cracked the hull open of this gig'. 'Right, showtime,' he continued.

'What? Really?' I said. 'Should we wait for a few others?'

'Well, it's already gone eleven at night. They'll be wanting their beds soon.'

I looked out at the enormous theatre – a thousand seats with thirty or so filled. Granted it was past the bedtime of many passengers, but with everyone I'd seen of free bus pass age, none of them would have to worry about getting back for the kids.

Vinod bounded onstage with his cheesiest smile and channelled his inner Yellowcoat. I never heard a 'Hi-de-hi!' but it was there in the subtext. He dealt with some jolly admin, told the gathered few dozen about upcoming tribute shows, salsa spectaculars and quiz nights, then ended his patter with a solemn gearshift:

'…And hey, if any of you are taken ill or are in any way queasy, don't forget to hop on down to Medical Bay! Especially if you're experiencing any symptoms of diarrhoea or vomiting. So without further ado …'

Wow. My big intro. Not only that, but peeking through the curtains I saw that one couple promptly left. Either they'd only come to hear the latest social, cultural and medical info, or one of them was definitely suffering those symptoms, and they thought best get to Medical Bay pronto. They couldn't risk what thirty minutes of Kerensic hilarity might do to them in such a fragile gastric condition.

In hindsight, they'd probably have coped fine, and in fact by scarpering to the nurse they dodged a bullet, show-wise. It wasn't my finest hour, it's fair to say. From the moment I first saw the drapes at the back of the auditorium sway to the ship's movement, to the final desperate pleas of 'Anyone here on Facebook?', I knew that this wasn't my night.

I could blame the low numbers, or the late hour, or the average age, or the large room, but I won't. I'll blame the doner kebab in pitta bread with chilli sauce from a certain van near junction 24 of the M1.

*   *   *

Sunday morning, 9.45 a.m., I think. We're on the nautical clock, so while it's definitely Sunday and I'm fairly sure it's morning, the time is probably four knots past Neptune or something.

I think we're off the coast of Portugal. Wherever we are, it's rocky, and we've been at sea for what seems like years, but is actually three days. I've eaten mostly oranges since we left Southampton, because of something I read about scurvy in History GCSE, or it might have been Biology, or that *Blackadder II* episode with Tom Baker in it. I'm still feeling queasy.

The only saving grace is that my work here is done, even if it went a little unlaughed-at. I tell myself that it wasn't my fault: it was under-attended, over-aged, and I was not over my takeaway.

I'm still not, but God willing I must feel better soon, if only because in another day I'll set foot on dry land. I want to take Spike Milligan's advice, and solve my seasickness by just sitting under a tree. That nearest tree will be Lisbon.

I've made a few ventures out of the cabin – I've tried the buffet, and it was an incredible feast. You could tell that most passengers had booked their holiday just for this. I've browsed the shopping mall, but don't fancy a ship in a bottle nor a diamond brooch for the pensioner in my life. I've walked around the pool deck, although refrained from a dip thanks to it being a bit gusty. I've even found that above the pool deck, there's a chapel.

So I've returned on Sunday morning for whatever service they provide, presumably featuring 'For Those in Peril on the Sea' and the Gospel reading of Jesus calming the stormy waters.

It's 9.55 a.m. and there's no one here. I know there is a religious service scheduled – the daily pamphlet told me so, along with the expected conditions of the day: the temperature would be low and the sea would be choppy, thanks for that. I've deduced it must be in the chapel, but I realise I've taken a punt on the time, so I wait it out. It's me, a roomful of twenty chairs, a cross on a table, and a view over the ocean waves. It's as calm as it's felt for three days, although I'm willing to put some of that down to being in the dead centre of the nineteenth and highest deck, which is perhaps a better place for balance than a cabin on the starboard side in the bowels of the ship.

At ten o'clock and with not so much as a lost holidaymaker, I abandon chapel, which is like abandoning ship but safer. I make for the information desk twelve decks down, and the glass lift reveals floor after floor of passengers reading, shopping and passing the time between breakfast and lunch. None headed for chapel but me, it seems.

'Bonjour, monsieur.'

I don't know why the concierge is adopting this accent. We were off the coast of France yesterday – he's a day behind. Unless he is actually French, which is more likely. Maybe all the concierges are French because 'concierge' is a French word. That would be nice: the maître d's – French; the matadors – Spanish; the sommeliers – Somalian.

'Hi, your chapel, is there a church service today?'

'Erm … let me check, monsieur.'

The concierge vanishes and after a conversation in Polish,[3] reappears to tell me the chapel is not used for church services.

'So why is there a chapel then?' I ask.

He pauses awkwardly and glances around. It's a tad tactless but I understand his less than subtle answer. Near us are two breathless ninety-year-olds, a man stooping so low that he's a walking right angle, and enough mobility scooters for it to look like the set of mid-nineties TV show *Robot Wars*. I root for all these people, but clearly the concierge's raise of the eyebrows indicates that sometimes passengers don't make it home. There are thousands of people on board this ship, and statistics alone mean that the chapel must be home to at least one or two impromptu funerals a year. I'm not saying they pick the instant 'burial at sea' option (although some might, to save on return luggage), but clearly a thanksgiving service is in order, or at least somewhere to pray for souls departed.

'We do have a Sunday morning Christian service, if you would like.'

'Ooh, yes please,' I reply.

'It's in the cinema, at half past ten.'

Of course, with a chapel on board, why wouldn't it be in the cinema?

I saunter slowly to the cinema to ensure a half-ten arrival, then quicken my speed when I realise that without a shuttle scooter, it's a long walk.

Once there, again I find myself alone. No co-worshippers, not even

---

[3] Now I don't know where I am.

any cinema-goers, although eventually a twelve-year-old – the youngest person I've seen in days – comes in to ask if *Madagascar 2* is showing yet. A poster tells him it starts at noon, and he leaves to go scrumping for apples, or whatever the scampish equivalent is at sea.

I take the ten-minute walk back to the information desk. This time I even ring the desk bell. I feel like Bernard Cribbins in that *Fawlty Towers* episode. I explain my woes, and the words sound odd: Christians aren't complainers, and basically I'm telling a waiter, 'Er, I ordered the church ...'

'Ah, the cinema manager may not have turned the projector on,' the concierge explains.

The projector? I assumed it was to be an in-person event, although I suppose yes, the ship is unlikely to employ a chaplain just for a Sunday service. The concierge explains to me that they have a non-denominational service pre-recorded on DVD. It gets repetitive if you're a worshipper on a cruise for several weeks, but it's better than nothing. Plus you can stay in your seats and watch animated lions at midday.

The concierge is yapped at in French and/or Polish, before finally telling me, 'If he is not there, we always show the service on channel 50 on your in-cabin TV.'

I retreat to my cabin for the last stop of my wild church chase. I recline on my unmade bed for the most laid-back church service I've ever 'attended'. I turn on the television and select channel 50. It's *Madagascar 2*.

I turn it off and consider my options. The chapel is empty. The cinema is empty. The Sunday service TV channel is showing a cartoon zebra. Catholics might for a second have heard the Gloria, before realising it's Gloria the Hippo.

There's no point troubling the concierge again, but I do have my iPod with me, and I've got a few sermons on there as podcasts, plus a browseable Bible on my phone. I've also got the odd worship song hidden among the Bananarama and Roxette (all eleven albums), so I search for 'God' and scroll through the *Godspell* soundtrack, *The Godfather* theme, and Kiss's 'God Gave Rock 'N' Roll To You' before finding an appropriate song to listen to. I start to wish I'd done the same with 'Heaven', as there's never a wrong time to listen to Heaven 17 and Belinda Carlisle.

So I recline on my bed and hold my own self-generated church service – a worship song or two, a talk from US speaker Tony Campolo, a read on the phone of some Bible quotes he uses and a few prayers of my own. It's all just for me and direct to my ears; it's an iChurch.

It feels very in touch with the digital age, but is it the future of Christianity? I hope not: it's very lonely. Communion's just not the same when you're faced with Garibaldi biscuits to cover both the bread and the wine. But it does go to show that just because a church is unavailable, you can still find some dedicated time if you seek it out.

All good services end with tea and something to entertain the kids, so I click on both the miniature kettle and channel 50. *Madagascar 2* is good medicine. I'm feeling better for the first time this trip, until I see a hippo singing 'I Like to Move It (Move It)', and the boat lurches to the right.

10

Pent Up

Praying with Pentecostals

As soon as I landed on sunny Guernsey, I could sense the island abuzz about the top comedian bringing them a show. Unfortunately that comedian wasn't me. While a top TV name was playing the thousand-seater hall, I'd be playing to a smaller audience as part of the same festival. Smaller in number but also in stature – it was a comedy club for kids.

It was bittersweet to see little five- and six-year-olds being walked up to the function room for my show. Part of me was panicking about the ensuing gig – what could I do that would entertain them? I didn't even know balloon-modelling.

The other part of me wept inside. I'd always known I'd have problems having kids, thanks to all sorts of medical nonsense since birth. I had been upfront with Zoë about it, but she'd married me anyway. I'd always passed the buck and changed the subject though, until now. Married and unpacked, we both turned our thoughts to the future. We'd keep trying, but with my dodgy innards, the docs reckoned our best bet was going to be IVF, adoption or dressing up a spaniel. I think he thought that would get a laugh from us, but there's a time and a place, mate.

IVF is expensive, so I had started taking every gig going, whether to grown-ups or littl'uns, or spaniels in drag. If it paid a wage, you could bet I'd give it a go. In confronting those issues at home though, it had the knock-on effect of a little broodiness out and about, especially when sweet angelic primary schoolers like these waddled on up to the venue.

In terms of show content, I made my peace with it: I'd entertain the parents and occasionally pull a silly face at the kids, plus I'd bought some Play-Doh. But they walked straight past my venue and into the neighbouring playground, causing me to wonder where my audience was? Then the noise hit me. Over the horizon, fifty marauding eleven-year-olds wreaked Godzilla-like havoc. I wanted a child, yes, but one that stopped at a cute age. I didn't want one of these monsters, currently charging into every car door in the car park. At least it took my mind off the IVF.

The show was a riot, almost literally. The parents at the edge of the room shook their heads in pity. Nothing was predictable. Jokes that I thought had a chance fell on stony ground. Set-ups that have never even tried to be funny suddenly earned gales of laughter because they mentioned words like 'cheese' or 'ferret', or best of all, 'cheese-ferret'.

I made them cheer for random things: cheer if you're a boy, cheer if you're Guernsian, cheer if you like biscuits, no I don't have any biscuits, no I'm not going to go and buy you some biscuits, no I can't bake you a biscuit, no I can't magic one from my nose, no I don't want one of your 'nose-biscuits', oh … cheese-ferret.

I tried crowbarring in regular material, and even just mentioning I had a wife caused the mob to shout, 'Divorce her! Divorce her!' More pitying looks came from parents, and I quietly sent back judging looks that they'd brought them here and brought them up to chant about divorce.

In the bar after the show, I nursed a two-in-the-afternoon stiff whisky, glasses hanging off my head, Play-Doh in my hair. It was so rare to finish a gig this early, so I planned the rest of my day. I'd swing by the show of the top TV name (who we'll call Buzz Hubbub, after all the commotion and general murmuring taking place on the island), to see what it's like when grown-ups laugh, but that left me with an afternoon. So I left the island.

I didn't go far, both geographically and in terms of my career, but I'd heard good things about the neighbouring island of Herm. It's tiny, you can walk around it in an hour or two, and I've always liked islands ever since I persisted with TV series *Lost*. Even six seasons of that didn't put me off.

I took the boat from Guernsey's balmy St Peter Port, and a short chug later stepped onto Herm's dock. The sun greeted us, and most tourists instantly hugged the coastline to sample the beaches. Some went straight for the island's only pub to sample the ale. I opted to go straight over the island's steep hill to sample a stitch and sunstroke. I began to regret the whisky.

Atop the island's centre, I found a tiny chapel dedicated to St Tugual. I wasn't familiar with him, but then I'd list my three most familiar saints as St Ivel, St Etienne and St John's Ambulance.

The chapel dates back a millennium, to when the Channel Islands were populated by priests, pacing the fields in their familiar brown coats.[1] Herm remains largely unchanged and unspoilt. There's one hotel, with no telephones, televisions or clocks. There's so little here that if you Google 'Things to do in Herm', the number one thing listed is 'Take a daytrip to Guernsey'. Yet that's the appeal.

I strode down to the other side of the island, a mere half-mile from where we'd docked. A sign read 'Belvoir Bay', and I felt as if I'd stepped through a portal into the Caribbean. Perhaps St Tugual was patron saint of *Quantum Leap*.

The cove at the base of the hill had everything: sun-kissed sand, crystal blue sea, the biggest yacht I've seen since *Howard's Way* ... and now me. I reclined on the sand, admired the view, continued to regret that whisky, and closed my eyes ...

I maintain that I never really slept – it's far too bright and I didn't have my eye mask. You wouldn't wear one on a beach anyway due to tan lines, or in my case, burn lines. I'd avoided the lines but alas not the burn. I really should have brought my ginger-only suncream. It was probably a good job that I wasn't onstage that night – I don't think my complexion could take the stage lights.

*　*　*

I slurped my iced water and felt it cool my face, as the intro announcement blared: 'Ladies and gentlemen, please welcome Misterrrrrrrrr Buzz Hubbub!'

I thought it was for me for a split-second, till I heard the name, and relaxed.

Buzz bounded onto the giant stage and I joined the thousand-strong audience in showing our appreciation. I maybe clapped a little more lightly, only because my hands still felt like they were on a barbecue.

I had heard chat about the show all day. When I went to buy some

[1] Or I may be thinking of cows.

aftersun[2] in St Peter Port's pharmacy, the man queuing behind me was on the phone trying to get tickets. When I was rehydrating with buckets of ice at dinner, the show was all neighbouring couples could talk about. I was fairly sure even 999 was diverting to voicemail tonight.

Now they were here, witnessing that guy from the telly, not him, you know, the other one. And he was delivering. Gag, local reference, gag, banter with front row, outrageous comment, gag, topical reference, mockery of people who didn't put suncream on today … It was textbook.

'So. There is no god.'

I wouldn't have got away with *that* at the kids' show.

His set-up was out there, and the audience waited on tenterhooks. A punchline didn't come immediately. Instead he repeated, 'There is no god.'

We waited again. The tenterhooks became uncomfortable.

Not only that, he told us, but all those who believe in a god, a soul, or any form of life after death, should stop wasting their time.

Something definitely changed among the audience. There was shifting in seats. Many were laughing along, but a nerve had been touched. Around me, I saw several couples with the general theme being the men continuing to chortle while the women weren't so sure.

As for me, I blushed. Or it could have been the sunburn.

As a Christian, I disagree. As a comedian, I'm used to hearing a wide range of opinions from the microphone: some true, some just for a laugh. I'm sure I've said countless things that people listening have disagreed with. And I know he's just telling us a joke, even if it is one that reflects his beliefs.

I'm often asked about where the line is in comedy, but I think the question is more: Is there a line? Is anything off-limits? In theory, a good comic likes to think they can tackle anything if there's wit and intellect involved. In practice, some subjects are more difficult than others. And above all, comedy has to come first.

Is it funny? That should be the overriding benchmark of any gag. There may be an opinion in the joke as well, whether it's a criticism of the Tory party, or of religion, or of a chicken's road-crossing tactics. But funny first, please.

Just like offensiveness though, funniness is subjective. So a comedian just has to do what they find funny, and hope the audience agrees. Over

---

[2] With cooling Aloe Vera.

time, a touring comedian will attract and detract punters, meaning they whittle down their audience to like-minded fans. You won't get many people at an Eddie Izzard show who don't like surreal flights of fancy, and if you go to a Tim Vine gig and don't like one-liners, you're an idiot.[3]

Buzz continued his onstage onslaught, and laughs came, but not as big as they could have been, and I'm sure not as big as they had been elsewhere. I had the sense that any discomfort wasn't just from churchgoers, but perhaps also from those on the fence. In that sense, at least Buzz's choice of subject matter may have helped, in some tiny way, push one or two people into an opinion.

Perhaps since the monks roamed the fields a thousand years ago, something of the spiritual has stuck in Guernsey. There are ten parish churches, plus buildings for every Christian denomination from Quakers to Catholics, to a geographically confusing Church of Scotland. There's even a gathering of Jehovah's Witnesses, who must find it tricky on the island: most people know each other so you'd probably recognise them coming up the drive: 'It's Malcolm again – turn the lights off ...'

There's no mosque or temple, and planning and space issues on the island mean there's unlikely to be either one. But Indian restaurants and Turkish kebaberies mean that employees with a faith need somewhere to pray, so there is a Muslim prayer room.

By the time Buzz had left the stage, he'd won many punters back, largely by moving on from religion. I had no problem with the subject matter, but if you don't agree with the set-up, then the punchline had better be pretty good. It's the same reason that I don't profess onstage, mid-routine, that there definitely is a God. The atheists in the room might get their hackles up, and then their heckles, and not much is funny after that. At least the believers in the audience tonight just stayed quiet, although I'm sure they were shouting prayers in their heads.

As I meandered back to the hotel, it's fair to say my face ached – partly through laughter, but largely as a reminder to pack suncream.

* * *

'Have you seen the sun?'

---

[3] Sorry to offend.

Wow, even for a Pentecostal church, asking on the way in if I've seen Jesus seems forward.

'Yes,' another woman chimes in. 'It was a scorcher yesterday, wasn't it?'

I realise that the only thing being evangelised about is factor 50, and make my way inside.

It's my first time in a Pentecostal church, and like some churchgoers at last night's show, this is a little outside of my comfort zone. I've had Guernsey's many churches to choose from, including the reputedly smallest chapel in the world, decorated entirely with broken china.

Or there was the simply-named 'Town Church', which claims to hold the odd record of being 'the UK's nearest church to a pub'. One of the church gargoyles apparently hangs suspiciously close to the gutter of the pub roof, like the gargoyle has his tongue out, trying in vain to lap up a bit of rogue ale that's somehow travelled up a drainpipe. It's a thankless task, thanks to gravity and being set in stone.

So, tempting as it was, proximity to booze sounded like the wrong reason to go to a church. Instead I've found myself here, for three main reasons:

- Last night's comedy prompts me not to huddle in with people of my own exact belief with my head in the sand, but to attempt openness with others, elsewhere in the faith.
- This church was nearest.
- My diary tells me that today is the seventh Sunday after Easter, aka the tenth day after Ascension Thursday, aka Whitsun, aka Pentecost.

Today is the birthday of the Church. Pentecost commemorates the Holy Spirit falling upon the disciples. It's the starting point of Christian believers spiritually meeting together, and is a day celebrated throughout the world in different ways:

- In France, they blow trumpets as the 'blowing of a violent wind' that accompanied the Spirit (Acts 2:2).
- In Italy, they scatter rose petals to signify the 'tongues of fire' (Acts 2:3).
- In England, we dress up with bells on our feet, bang sticks

together and roll cheese down hills, maybe because of a few verses later: 'Some made fun of them and said, "They have had too much wine."' (Acts 2:13).

Here in the Pentecostal church, it looks like business as usual – a nearly-full meeting of families, all cheery and all cheery and sun-drenched. I'm a little broody again, till some more pre-teen ogres come tearing in.

The building itself looks like a modern take on a traditional church: one stained-glass window, a slightly raised stage area, a vaulted ceiling. Yet everything feels stripped down. Other churches would be tempted to fill the walls with posters, banners and Bible verses, but here there's more wall-space, and more focus. There's the merest hint of Ikea.

I'm instantly spotted as new; not a surprise on an island such as this. They must have reached the point where new blood doesn't so much come from brand new Christians, as people defecting from the Church of Scotland up the road.

I browse the bookshelf near the back, hoping to gain some quick last-minute insights into the Pentecostal way. A leaf through tells me that although traditions here may be different to my church, many of the customs have been making their way to Anglican churches for years ...

Pentecostals and friends – a handy guide
aka A Colossal Glossary of Glossolalia

Gifts of the Spirit: These aren't general 'gifts from God' ('Ooh, the way he kicks a football/sculpts ice/folds napkins into swans – it's a gift from God ...'). These are words of wisdom, prophecies, the ability to speak in tongues, and various other divine gifts outlined in 1 Corinthians 12. It goes on to say that the greatest gift is love, in the familiar 'Love is patient, love is kind' reading heard at weddings (where you'll also find napkins folded into swans). It's the only time gifts and weddings are so closely thought of without the gifts including a set of bath towels and a sandwich toaster.

Glossolalia: Speaking in tongues. It may sound like babbling to the uninitiated, but glossolalists see their words as a gift from the Spirit, either to be interpreted, or to be left untranslated in its pure form. Saying the word 'glossolalists' is not an example of speaking in tongues, though can sound like it.

Cessationists/Continuationists: 'Will wonders never cease?' Well yes, cessationists think they mostly have ceased. Continuationists, such as Pentecostals, charismatics and neo-charismatics, think they carry on.

Pentecostalism: A church that emphasises baptism in the Holy Spirit as a crucial part of a relationship with God, separate from conversion itself. With this spiritual baptism come the gifts of the Spirit, as opposed to a water baptism where the gift is normally a Bible or book tokens.

Charismatic movement: The movement of some mainstream churches to more Pentecostal practices. Born (or born again) in the 1960s, charismatics wanted to practise what the Pentecostals had seen as spiritual gifts, but remain part of a mainstream church. Unlike Pentecostalism, charismatics wanted to use these gifts to renew their own churches, rather than break off and start anew. The Protestant Church had its charismatic revival in the early 1960s, and the Catholic Church in the late 1960s, but the Evangelical Church held off until 1985, when the evangelical/charismatic mix became known as ...

Neo-charismatics: Nothing to do with Keanu Reeves in *The Matrix*. Not quite Pentecostals (the First Wave), not quite charismatic (the Second Wave), yet today the Third Wave is bigger than both combined. Their services are full of prophecy, speaking in tongues, and laying-on of hands. The difference from the pentes and charismos is less stress on being baptised in the Spirit to receive these gifts. It's much more 'in the moment' than being prepared for that moment with spiritual baptism. So you can just turn up and immerse yourself. These churches are relatively new, in new buildings, with little or no tradition, so don't expect church organs, dog collars or stained-glass windows. Do expect doughnuts.

'Good morning!' thunders a man from behind me. Any impression of a library-like atmosphere is now gone. The resonating voice causes a book to wobble and fall off its shelf.

I turn to see a grey-haired man in a suit. I smile and hope he's not another one to comment on my peeling face, so I steer the conversation by quickly saying, 'Hello, I'm just visiting.'

'Oh. Righto!'

I'm sure I detect a hint of annoyance that I'm not a local Baptist changing sides. I explain I'm just here for one day, and he winces as if to say, 'All right, don't labour it.'

'You on holiday?' he enquires, standing needlessly close for such a voice. He's clearly a Shakespearean actor who missed his calling.

I tell him about the comedy festival, and try not to mention the kids' show. But he asks exactly what show I've been doing here, so I tell him about my role yesterday afternoon as babysitter/punchbag.

'Oh! I must introduce you to Simon and Heather. Do you know them? Of course not.' He gives a little chuckle, knowing that he too could be a comedian if he wanted to. 'Heather! Simon!' His voice shakes the room. 'Come and meet our friend ...'

'... Paul ...' I say.

'He's a ...'

Don't say children's party entertainer. I'm not a children's party entertainer.

'... comedian.'

Thanks.

The bellowing gent turns back and takes a full view of me.

'You don't look like a clown!' he says wryly. 'No oversized shoes. No red ...'

He looks directly at my sunburnt nose, and stops talking.

'Heather! Come, meet Paul!'

Heather and Simon, she thirty, he forty, are working their way across the room. I fill the void by asking the booming man about himself, a little belatedly. He introduces himself as David, a Guernsey resident for twenty years. He's been part of this church for six, and is an interpreter.

'Oh really?' I reply with interest. I assume this close to France, there's great demand for his work. 'What languages? Would that be French ...?'

'Tongues.'

A lesser man would snigger.

It takes a few seconds to understand what he means, till I realise that he wasn't telling me his job, but his role in church. When others prophesy in tongues, which to untrained ears would sound like babbling, David may be able to interpret the message.

It's here that I see the difference between this Pentecostal church and churches I've visited that have drawn on Pentecostal practices. Elsewhere, very occasionally, I've heard people praying in tongues, or singing worship songs which then become this different language. It's often left un-interpreted, a direct communication from worshipper to worshippee.[4] Sometimes the speaker might interpret their own sounds after they've returned to recognisable speech. Sometimes others may step forward and give impressions of what they felt the Spirit was saying. Here, people like David actually have the specific job of interpreting what's being said. Any French visitors will have to fend for themselves.

My mind races to whether there are courses that enable you as an interpreter. Are there Berlitz phrasebooks, or a Rosetta Stone audio course you can listen to on car journeys? I somehow doubt it, but David is in no doubt as to his skills. Believe it or not, but he does.

Heather and Simon have pushed their way through the minglers, and just reach us when the minister begins the service.

As we are about to find seats, David leans in to the three of us commandingly. 'Paul's a stand-up comedian,' he shout-whispers to Heather and Simon. And to me: 'Heather and Simon went to a comedy show last night.'

I find a seat feeling Heather and Simon's uncertain look towards me. They're not quite sure what to make of me. But then, much as I'm here with an open mind, the feeling is probably mutual.

The minister welcomes us warmly, and saves a particular welcome

[4] i.e. God.

for me, the first-timer. 'Always nice to see new faces,' he says. I'm not sure if he just means he's never seen a skin tone this crimson before.

It's a good service for a first-timer, as he uses the occasion of Pentecost to retrace the biblical origins of the spiritual gifts. As a result the introduction becomes a Bible reading then a mini-sermon, as the minister takes us on a tour of Acts 2 and 1 Corinthians 14, drawing out the specific verses that point to the use of prophecy and words of wisdom. These then empower us, he says, to go forth from here into Christian service, which tomorrow includes running a community day. Wow: intro, reading, sermon and now notices, all rolled into one. These folks really get it all out of the way up top.

A time of sung worship is introduced, and the band takes the stage. It's a good size for this relatively small building, and the drummer has to hide behind a giant barrier. Clearly when he gets going, he deafens people.

And they do indeed get going. We sing traditional songs, but at a pace, and I'm sure it quickens as we sing. All across the congregation, arms are raised and hands are thrown into the air. I join in a little, when the music feels right, but I'm incredibly self-conscious, both as a newbie and as a Church of Englander. It seems I can humiliate myself in front of children for half an hour, yet not let go in a roomful of strangers, who are all letting go themselves.

The music fades and the minister smoothly links into further notices, while many gradually come down from the sung worship.

'So don't forget our special community day tomorrow,' the minister says.

A voice from the front echoes him. 'Tomorrow, yes ...'

I'm used to churches where the vicar speaks and we don't. Here, everyone joins in. The minister continues:

'So if you can help with sandwiches ...'

'Yes ... cheese and pickle ...'

'I think we've got cheese and pickle covered actually.'

'Ham and mustard, yes, ham and mustard ...'

And so it continued. Pentecostal responses are not just for singing and praying, it seems.

We're invited to greet others – the equivalent of the Anglo-Catholic 'Peace be with you' – and told that this will merge into a five-minute break. I've sat alone in my row, so turn around to greet my nearest neighbours and discover for the first time that Heather and Simon are sitting behind me.

We remake acquaintance, and Heather breezily asks if I'm here for the comedy festival. I tell her that I am, tell them about the kids' show, and explain that it's not my usual gig.

'So you do churches?' Simon asks.

'Sometimes,' I reply. 'But normally just pubs and clubs – the comedy circuit.'

This surprises them. I think after last night, they can't comprehend what a churchgoer might have to say at a regular comedy night. Heather nervously asks about my act, and I do my best to describe it, in a way that will hopefully stop her from saying, 'Tell us a joke then.' Because in these circumstances, away from a microphone and an audience, they just don't work. Often even with a microphone and an audience, they just don't work.

'I was at the show last night,' I report, and Simon raises his eyebrows.

'Oh!' says Heather. 'I don't know that it was for us. We were a bit shocked.'

Simon nods, and I tell them that I do see a place in comedy for the edgy and non-edgy alike. There'll always be comics wanting to push the limits of acceptability, and there will always be an audience for that. Equally, I hope there'll always be an audience for acts that just want to give punters a good time.

As edgy comics get edgier, more jump on the bandwagon to break more taboos. So the boundaries change, and the middle ground shifts with it – the 'norm' changes. So I urge Simon and Heather not to be put off comedy after last night. By all means if they want to vote with their feet, they can, just don't leave comedy clubs altogether. The comedy business is, like all free market economies, a democratic one, so I encourage them to stick with it. Without more mainstream comedians, the edgier ones will have nothing to react against. We feed each other.

It's a tough ask, but I hope they'll give the comedy world another go. I can see why they didn't like the topic of religion introduced in the way it was. Being confronted at a comedy night with, 'There is no God,' is like being confronted with, 'Your wife doesn't exist'. Whether or not you agree with it, it's going to provoke you, when you just want a laugh. Some comics want to provoke, which is all fine and dandy – sometimes I want to provoke too. But we have to be aware of the silences and puttings-off that may follow.

There's a silence between Heather, Simon and I, so I wonder if I've still put them off comedians. Simon breaks it: 'Lot of atheists in comedy though, aren't there?'

'Well there are a lot of atheists everywhere,' I reply. I try and get across that God needn't be taboo. I speak of how the Robin Inces and Marcus Brigstockes of this world have brought wit and verve and laughs to the subject of religion. And I tell them how the unfortunate spillover means some new acts I've gigged with have tried to get a cheap laugh by writing off Jesus as a fictional character, with no real follow-up. It's galling not just as a Christian but as a comedian, and smacks of lazy bandwagon-jumping. It means when I go on after them, I want to talk about religion in a positive – yet non-preachy – way. The overriding impetus though should always remain: Be funnier, be better. A rant back will not do.

We're cut short as the minister restarts. I feel something under my feet, and see that Heather's kicked her shoes off. She knows what's coming.

It's a time of lively musical worship again, with a variety of sung ad-libs. Most people are adding their own notes, sounds and occasionally lyrics. If I'm singing an E-flat, there'll be a B-flat sung out from the row in front somewhere. I hear the harmonies, and wonder if they practise, together, ahead of Sunday worship – it sounds that well-rehearsed. Yet I know it's not. For these people, the power of Spirit moves among them. And we've only just got going ...

The music plays as an instrumental under the prayers, and we're asked if anyone has anything particular they wish to have mentioned. I consider our ongoing fertility ponderings, but decide to leave it between me, my wife and God. Prayers here are very communal, and sure enough after each one is offered, people join in with various 'Amen's and 'Yes Lord's. I hear no 'Alleluia's, but that would be a bit of a walking, singing, dancing stereotype.

The minister preaches some more, again celebrating today as the anniversary of both the church's birth and of speaking in tongues. David is standing by, ready to interpret. The minister invites us, if we want to renew our faith today, if we want to be healed, emotionally, spiritually or phsyically, to come down to the front as the next songs play. The altar call.

We sing two more songs, and by the second one, the momentum is gathering. The band play and replay and the congregation take the words and run with them.

Many, like me, are taking a more tranquil approach. Not all are carried away into the ecstatic next level of worship. Perhaps half are motionless, and half are going full pelt, with arms raised, some now dancing in the aisles – with shoes off – and one or two are now crying.

Mid-sentence, the worship leader breaks off and moves to the front, and the minister and other elders lay hands upon her. The band keeps playing without her, but the singing stops abruptly. She leads the worship, and she has decided that the singing stops here, for now.

One tall man has joined the worship leader at the foot of the stage, and various others including Simon have gone to lay their hands on him. The minister gives me a fleeting look to see if I want to join; I pass.

The tall man begins to babble, then rock on the floor, and then most surprising of all: outrageous laughter. For minute after minute, he guffaws, chortles, snorts, hoots and cackles. After five minutes he's holding his aching sides, and after ten he's literally rolling in the aisles. Most of those attending to the worship leader have now gathered around the tall man – he needs their help more. He's a big man, and six adults now flank him, for his own protection. He has eyes closed and is still laughing uproariously, and without these guards, his flailing could take out a good couple of rows.

Some children have come through from their Sunday school to take a look, and the minister reassures them.

I have no idea if his laughter is any way linked to the comedy festival being in town, but I know for sure that it's the most laughter I've heard anyone emit for years. That probably says more about my career than it does about anything.

It's a totally experiential moment. You're either in it or you're not, and I feel slightly like I'm looking in through the sole stained-glass window (although I'd need a big ladder).

It strikes me that in the last twelve hours I've seen two sets of people talking on stages, and I like both sets; I warm to them. With one I share a comedic take on the world, and a care for the free speech of artists. With the other I share their Christian beliefs, even though their practices seem at odds with my experiences. I'm not quite on the same page as either group, and I feel that I've opted for 'the middle way'. I admire the passion of both comedian and church: something that us middle-grounders often find difficult to put into words, since by our nature, we're trying to keep the peace.

The service draws to an official close, but is gradual in finishing: the tall man is still laughing in the aisle, and being firmly restrained by a handful of the congregation's toughest blokes. Children are still looking on, wide-eyed. The worship leader rejoins her band for some closing quiet music. Conversations recommence, including three kind invitations for me to come to lunch. In all my years of church-hopping, I've never had so many offers in one go. It's a shame that I'm heading off the island shortly, because I'm a big fan of lunch, and I'm an even bigger fan of three lunches.

I leave the church, as many continue to mingle, shoes off. Some are still praying, one is still laughing. David stands at the door, quite jolly despite the fact that his interpretation has not been needed. I bid him *au revoir*, and take a last look at the people who have been, as the minister implied, filled up and refuelled for Christian service.

I follow Simon and Heather – now with shoes – out into the glorious day, and sunburn instantly pains me. I've felt welcomed today, even though my traditional background makes me feel like a visitor rather than one of the family.

I nod a goodbye to them, and we all walk down the same achingly sunny street. Some passers-by walk in the opposite direction while I walk in the shade, and Simon and Heather choose to walk in the sun.

11

Melting Pot

Conversing in Cafés

Edinburgh Festival: the hills too steep, the rent too steep, yet once again I found myself back for another financial gamble. It came with domestic decisions about a festival fund versus a fertility fund, but with a thousand pounds outlaid on the Fringe before discussion had even begun, I've ended up here. Besides, I'm not the only one taking a chance.

Some people make an annual trip to Vegas to lose money on the poker tables; for comedians, it's this beautiful city. There's architecture and landscape here that you never think possible in this country, in this century. For the tenth year in a row, I found my accommodation in a gorgeous Georgian townhouse, on the top floor. It was a five minute stair-climb, since each Edinburgh apartment seems to have vaulted ceilings so high you wonder if they're built to accommodate cabers. One day Stannah stairlifts will get a contract to fit out this entire city, and that will be a happy day.

My show venue was similarly archaic, and still under construction. It had walls and a ceiling, but was currently a cave. That's not a metaphor: it was a literal cave. The Edinburgh Fringe is known for using every possible space as a venue. Be it a school, a car park or a public toilet, someone will have tried to fit a row of seats in there and charge a tenner a ticket for entry. It seemed now that every actual building had been used, so yes, I was put in a cave. I had metaphorically ridden to the Edinburgh Fringe office on my donkey full of props, only to be told there was no room at the inn, but try the muddy stable, and that'll be three thousand pounds please.

Given nature began work on my cave venue several thousand years ago, I was a little confused to be told by venue staff that it wasn't built yet.

'Give us an hour,' said a student with purple glasses. It struck me that if you have purple glasses, building an entertainment venue is probably not your forte.

'You know my show starts in three hours?' I checked.

'Then we'll have two hours free,' came the sharp reply.

I asked him where I could put my props box, currently containing a dozen wigs, two extendable mops and a full Santa outfit. It was August, but it was the Fringe, so none of this looked out of place. In fact the only odd thing was that I didn't have purple glasses. After some confusion over whether we'd have room for props storage even when the venue was finished, I decided to give him that hour and plodded off with my metaphorical donkey.

I used the time to put up posters and hand out flyers ahead of my show – the Edinburgh exhaustion comes not from performing but from pitching to the thousands of people who have thousands of shows to consider. Prop box at my feet, I started to flyer passersby, and before long found I'd given a flyer to a comedian I know called Dan.

'Waiting for my venue to be ready,' I explained, gesturing to the box of wigs. 'Looks like we may not get storage space.'

'Yeah, you don't want to lug that back and forth every day,' Dan empathised. 'Although you could wear the wigs and dress as Santa. What are the other shows in your venue doing with their stuff?'

'I dunno. Maybe they have no stuff, and just need a cave wall. Maybe they're dramatic retellings of potholing adventures.'

'No props, no frills for me this year,' said Dan. 'Me and a mic. Even left my guitar at home.' I didn't even know he played guitar. 'I'd give you a flyer, but "my people" have got them all. They're getting some posters up.'

Oh to have 'people'. Granted, you needed to have been on a few TV panel shows, or in Dan's case, be prepared to go into debt by ten thousand pounds, but on the plus side he got to look smug all month and talk about 'his people'.

With nothing better to do, Dan wandered with me back to my cave, which looked identical to when I'd left it two hours ago.

'We've been trying to unfurl this banner,' explained Purple Glasses. 'And we think we've got WiFi working.' I knew it would be great comfort to the audience, unaided by lights or seats, that the banner outside the cave was well unfurled. They'd probably blog about it using the WiFi.

Dan helped me carry a few chairs into the 'auditorium', finding it fun to muck in since he wasn't doing any work on his own production. One hour later, my show's start time came, and it almost looked like a theatre. A dank cavernous theatre, but a theatre.

I made my way 'backstage', and unfortunately couldn't peer through the curtain to spy on the audience coming in due to a lack of curtains, and a lack of audience. This being a cave, I peeked behind a jutting rock instead. With no sign even saying this was a venue, I expected no one but lost palaeontologists. Amazingly the audience, like the underground spring water to my left, started to seep in. These were the dedicated few, who wouldn't be put off by no signs or box office. They'd trip over power cables and guess a route through the cave corridors. One unfurled banner lying on the ground reading 'Edinburg' and a strong WiFi signal was all they needed to know that comedy lay within.

An Edinburgh first night
A to-do list to make a bad show

- Make sure you accelerate through it – that way they may miss jokes and you'll be done early.
- Forget chunks of material. It may make no sense without that earlier set up, but hey, make the audience do some work.
- Deviate off-topic thanks to heavy machinery outside. Those roads won't fix themselves, and you may discover you're an improv genius. Or just lose your place.
- Latecomers: pander to their every need. How dare you start on time.
- Fend off leaks from above, because all good venues are made of rock, and all good performers bring an umbrella onstage.
- Brought wigs, a Santa outfit, and some mops? Why not forget to use any of them? Besides, the mops may come in handy for the pool of water onstage, thanks to that unforeseen stalactite.

As the sixteen stalwarts of my opening night audience filed out, I took a sigh of relief at being $\frac{1}{24}$ of the way through the festival. It was to be a long month, and I knew I had to keep my vitamins up, but just for one night I thought I'd try the local delicacy of kebab pizza, opting for the healthy option by not having it deep-fried.

Kebab pizza down to crust and bones, I found myself outside a modern church building, advertising a drop-in zone for fringe-goers. I was a fringe-goer, so I dropped in. The conversation that followed was like a scene from a festival play, which I'll call *Same God, Different Church*:

NAZ: Hi, I'm Naz.
PAUL: Thanks. Paul.
NAZ: Do you want a napkin?
PAUL: Sorry?
NAZ: You've got a bit of chilli sauce just ...

PAUL dabs his chin with a napkin.

NAZ: Enjoying the festival?
PAUL: Yeah. I'm doing a show.
NAZ: Yeah? Like a play?
PAUL: A stand-up show. Comedy.
NAZ: Right. That's good. God likes to laugh. Do you know God?
PAUL: I'm an Anglican.
NAZ: Oh okay. Do you know God?
PAUL: Yeah, I do.
NAZ: Oh. Okay. Cool. I might try and make it to some shows. You never know what you're going to get though, do you?
PAUL: Well you don't, but that's part of the fun, isn't it?
NAZ: I don't know. I saw a show a few years ago – the comedy was quite edgy. The F word, the S word, the D word ...
PAUL: (*Thinks*) What's the D word? (*Says*) Looks like a nice church.
NAZ: Yeah, it's great. I've been here for five years, came here as a student. Evangelical, God-shaped community.
PAUL: What shape's that?
NAZ: (*Quick as a flash*) A heart shape.
PAUL: Nice.
NAZ: Have you ever done an Alpha course?

PAUL: No, but ...

NAZ: You should do an Alpha course. Our church hosts our next one in September.

PAUL: I live in Guildford.

NAZ: Is that near Morningside?

PAUL: A bit further south. Every August I decamp to Edinburgh.

NAZ: Decamp?

PAUL: Decamp.

NAZ: I've heard of those courses. In America. Do they work?

PAUL: Eh?

NAZ: Is 'post-gay' the right term?

PAUL: I meant just ... forget the 'decamp' thing. I travel to Edinburgh every August.

NAZ: Oh. Right. Well if you're only here for the festival, there's the Café Church on Sunday evening. It's not part of this church, but could be good if you're just interested in Christianity.

PAUL: I'm Anglican.

NAZ: Yeah. I hear the café do free jammie dodgers.

NAZ gives PAUL a flyer. PAUL takes it.

PAUL: I'd better give you a flyer for my show. No jammie dodgers I'm afraid.

PAUL attempts to give NAZ a flyer. NAZ eventually takes it.

PAUL: Well I better go. It's been lovely.

NAZ: Hasn't it? Hope to see you Sunday. And do drop in here any time. Open late each night for the fringe-goers.

PAUL: How late?

NAZ: I think till 9pm.

PAUL: Well, bye.

NAZ: Wait, can I pray for you first?

NAZ prays for PAUL. PAUL says a quick prayer back, because it would have been rude not to. NAZ and PAUL both open their eyes and shoo away a CROWD who thinks it's a fringe show.

PAUL: Well, bye, Naz.

NAZ: Bye, Paul.

PAUL: (*to CROWD*) Seriously, please go.

Exit PAUL, pursued by CROWD.

Three days and three shows later, I'd had two reviews: a four-star write-up that read like a three-star, and a three-star that read like a child's essay. I'd had two rainy afternoons flyering (one star – 'a wash-out') and a deep-fried cheeseburger (five stars – 'a visceral sensation that hits you in the gut'). There is a tendency here to review everything, I thought as I read my three-star review again, then rated the review one star, then rated my review of it five stars.

I heard a familiar voice across the street.

'Hey, Kerensa!' It was Dan again, discussing with one of 'his people' just how big he'd like his face to appear in the next print run of posters. I crossed to see him, and we decided to grab a 6 p.m. lunch (Edinburgh timings meant breakfast at noon and dinner at midnight). We sought jacket potatoes – mine just cheese, his coronation chicken, because his show was selling out. And while I'd had a three- and a four-star review, he'd had the same but three of each. We were both average, but his averageness was more highly publicised thanks to his top PR team.

It turned out that his show wasn't the only thing selling out, but jacket potatoes were too. With none left, they'd closed early, so we meandered on. We passed a centuries-old church, converted into a theatre for the month, and currently pounding out R&B. A chalkboard showed that now performing was *Riot! The Musical*.

'Wow, Christians are funky!' said Dan with a dash of sarcasm.

'Yeah, we are,' I agreed.

'Ha! Oh, are you a ... you're one of them? Oh no.'

'Yes Dan,' I replied testily.

Dan took a step back from me, as if to check I was a Christian from my head to my toes. 'I thought you liked science and maths and things?'

'Can I not like both? Can I not say God created science and maths and things, and aren't they good?'

He handed me a flyer. 'You should really come see my show. I've got this bit in it about rationalists versus you guys.'

I took his flyer out of habit, then offered it back. 'No offence, Dan, but if three years studying Theology, the existence of fossils, and the existence of Richard Dawkins, all can't stop me believing what I believe, then I doubt five minutes of shtick about God-botherers is going to get me putting my Bible on eBay.'

Dan returned his flyer in his back pocket. 'It's your funeral. After which you're dead in the ground.'

There was silence between us.

'You've gone quiet,' said Dan.

'Just saying a prayer for you,' I replied. He didn't look happy about that.

'Yeah, well listen to this silence …' Dan replied, followed by a few seconds pause throughout which his stomach rumbled. 'I need food,' he conceded. 'Just a biscuit or something.'

'Do you like jammie dodgers?' I asked.

'Heck, yeah.'

And off we went to Café Church.

* * *

En route I explain to Dan about the concept of Café Church. I don't want to pull the wool over the eyes of this lost sheep (now there's an image). Dan rolls his eyes but gives it his blessing.

'As long as they do jammie dodgers, I'm in,' he says.

We arrive at the café, and to my surprise it is a bona fide café – the difference is that it should be closed for business, but it's occupied by a group of Christians with a mic stand and a guitar, like a band of survivors in those apocalyptic films who break into and occupy deserted shops.

'Glad you could make it, Mr Comedian.' It's Naz from the drop-in.

'Comedians,' I correct, and introduce Dan.

Dan puts his hand out. 'Hello, I'm Dan. Non-believer.' He then scans the room for jammie dodgers, spies them and nudges me. We edge towards them – this is our dinner. The room now has a dozen or so people, and most haven't spotted the biscuits.

A young woman greets the room via microphone: 'Hi everyone, I'm Jeanette, thanks for coming. Do grab a coffee and a seat, or mill around, or whatever. I'm going to play a song while you come in, and then Ian's going to say a hello after that.'

She spends a minute tuning up her guitar and then sings an unfamiliar song, which has the unfortunate consequence of raising the volume of everyone's conversations. Dan and I give her our full attention – we're performers so know what it's like, and besides we're busy munching. By the time she finishes, Dan and I have had a fine banquet of jammie dodgers. We're trying to justify the jam as part of our five-a-day, but our stomachs ache and disagree.

A chap in a lumberjack shirt tries to bring the room to order. He introduces himself as Ian, Jeanette's husband. Ian and Jeanette – they don't look like The Krankies, but have the names and the accents.

'Great to see you if it's your first time at our café. We're going to have just an informal chat really. Now I'm a Christian, but I don't want to speak Christianese here tonight. Let me just read you a short passage from the New Testament – that's the second one ... '

He reads a passage from Mark's gospel, the Parable of the Growing Seed.

'Now to make it interesting – well not interesting, it *is* interesting – to make it different, I'm going to give a little talk, but I'm going to incorporate some words, which you've all been writing on slips of paper by the biscuit plate.'

I didn't notice any paper; in fact I'm worried we might have eaten it. Dan leans over and speaks in a hush, 'Don't worry, I've got this covered. Look out for "Barcelona".'

Uh oh. This should be unusual: a sermon improvised around suggestions from the audience. Very 'Edinburgh'.

'So,' begins Ian, the bowl of paper slips by his side. 'We're told the Kingdom of God grows like a seed, so whether you believe or not ... ' He reads a piece of paper. '... Snow-leopards. Can a snow-leopard change its spots? Does a snow-leopard have spots? There's a question.'

I'm not sure about this. He's already going off-topic.

'... But the seed grows, in its time, like a ...' Another piece of paper. '... bungalow. You might say that bungalows don't grow, but I'd say to you ...' Another. '... Thanks for the jammie dodgers ...'

A man to my left with crumbs in his beard looks pleased with himself.

'Actually that slightly misses the point of the exercise ...'

The bearded man frowns.

'But let's get back to the seed ...'

Let's.

'… That seed grows, and God's kingdom grows, and we're part of that. God wants us in it. You may feel pushed away. You may feel unworthy. You may feel totally unspiritual. But the important thing is …' He picks up a slip. '… Humphrey Bogart.' And another. 'And trams.' Yet another. 'In Barcelona.'

Dan punches the air with an 'Olé!' on that word, as if he's the victim of a cruel hypnotist.

It was a bold idea, and was kind of fun. We've had a laugh, and we've learnt something, if only that improv sermons may not be a thing of the future.

Ian wrapped up the event. 'You know what, I'd love it if we could just pray now, for a minute, maybe, if there are no objections? Yeah? I mean only if we're all okay with that?'

I look around. No objections. You have to tread lightly at Café Church, I imagine. Some may be here to worship, some to find out more about Christianity, some for the coffee.

So we pray, and Ian concludes by adding, 'One suggestion for those who like to pray, maybe for yourselves, maybe for your loved ones. How about opening a phone book, picking a random person, and praying for them? Wouldn't that be great?'

One or two teens among us look uncertain – I don't think they know what a phone book is.

As the meeting disbands, we're encouraged to mingle and Naz joins us with a coffee.

'So what did you think?' he asks Dan and me. He clearly sees us both as newbies, Dan the atheist and me the Anglican.

I tell him I've enjoyed it; it's been unthreatening and diverting, although I secretly missed having more of a focal point. I liked Ian's idea of phone book praying – I'm certainly guilty of praying mostly for myself and my loved ones. So I've definitely taken something away from this.

Dan takes a deep breath before giving his verdict. Naz and I don't know what to expect. Dan finally comes out with, 'Let me get a coffee.' And he throws his coat next to Naz's chair.

I make my excuses and leave them to it for my evening show. As I reach the door I see Dan and Naz deep in chat and caffeine. I hear Dan talk of 'Dawkins' and Naz talk of 'Hitchens', and anticipate their conversation being a feisty one. This could be the beginning of a beautiful friendship, in the words of Humphrey Bogart, on a tram, in Barcelona.

I do like informal church. I've had some great sessions of 'Beer & Hymns' at Greenbelt Festival at Cheltenham Racecourse: two hundred people belting out 'Jerusalem' and 'Guide Me, O Thou Great Redeemer' while swilling ale. Messy Church is marvellous for all the family, and does exactly what it says on the tin. Then there's Pub Church, Café Church, Park Church, House Church ... It's like Edinburgh Festival venues. At the Fringe you can find shows in caves, toilets and even churches. It's equally true that across the UK you can find churches in cafés, bars and flats. It's odd that the church down the road hosts *Riot! The Musical* while this church meets in a café, but many of the people here wouldn't come if it were in a traditional church building.

I'd encourage Naz into a comedy club and Dan into a church. It's a good thing that these folks set foot in this café, just as I'm sure it's good that punters down the road are setting foot in a church, even if it is to see a musical featuring songs like 'Don't Kettle Me In, Mr Policeman'. At least I think that's a good thing.

I leave and see a poster of Dan's face with four stars plastered over it. Which makes me reflect on where I've just been ...

Event 4/5, Coffee 4/5, Biscuits 5/5. My stomach hurts.

12

Work in Progress
Meeting with Methodists

'I'm pregnant. We're going to have a baby.'

These words change everything, especially if you barely recognise the person speaking. Thankfully on this occasion, it was my wife.[1]

Our prayers had been answered. It was around about the time my hand was wavering over the cheque book for IVF. We gave thanks, a lot, and Zoë did pregnancy tests, a lot.

After a few days of disbelief and staring at lines on test kits, the responsibility set in. I realised I'd need to work twice as hard. The next Edinburgh Festival fund – to blow a small fortune on performing a fringe show to nine people – became the baby fund. When it came to the choice of printing a thousand flyers or buying a thousand nappies, I had to choose the nappies. You can't wrap a child's bottom in a picture of my face, or at least I wouldn't want to.

We still couldn't quite believe it, till the bump showed itself. Watching a lot of *Dragon's Den* at the time, we nicknamed the bump 'Theo the Foetus'. We knew though that 'Theo the Baby' wouldn't work in the same way, so we started looking elsewhere for inspiration. Biblical names have always been popular whether you're religious or not, from David to Daniel to Mary to Matthew. I shortlisted Pontius, Methuselah and Herod, and Zoë unshortlisted them.

As bump started to grow, I started to grow up. I saw the world in different ways. I'd mutter at underdressed clubbers that they'd catch their death, and how no daughter of mine would go out dressed like that. Tuition fees went from being a financial bullet I'd dodged, to being a barrier to little Methuselah's education in twenty years' time. I was becoming the sort of person who couldn't read a newspaper without grumbling.

---

[1] For clarity, that's been the only occasion I've heard those words.

So it was probably apt that an email came in to prick my conscience. It was a charity called Operation Noah, asking if I would write a stand-up set on the subject of climate change awareness. I told them climate change was quite a dry subject matter, and they said there's joke number one. I said the subject would need a few ice-breakers, and they said there's joke number two. And so it continued.

The idea of making jokes about fossil fuels was a little alien to me, but then so was parenthood. Any minute now, the only comfort zone I'd be experiencing would be the tea area in a soft play centre. And what better way to focus your mind on a future for your children's children than expecting children. So I started reading about the world of climatology, sceptics, deniers and activists, and started writing about it.

Armed with the clunky ...

'A climate change sceptic walks into a bar, asks for a strong whisky. But 98% proof isn't enough for him, and there's isn't any ice left.'

... and ...

'Knock knock. Who's there? The sea.'

... and even ...

'My wife's gone to the West Indies. Obviously she's taken a boat because flying long-haul is damaging, even when offsetting carbon emissions.'

... I hit the delete key and started again.

I've always liked fairly straightforward jokes. When people ask for my comic heroes, I don't pick the comedians' favourites, like maverick satirist Bill Hicks, great as he was. I go for Bob Monkhouse. He had jokes, and yes he had game shows too, but principally he was a walking gagopaedia.

So in considering my task, I channelled Monkhouse. As a gag-writer for hire, I like the challenge of finding jokes about any given subject matter, with a good amount of time on Wikipedia and a few comedic crowbars. I've written for Radio 4's *The Now Show* and *The News Quiz*, where some weeks the news would give us David Blaine sitting in a box above the Thames, but often the news was less helpful. The writers' room would fill with dread when the producer arrived with the words, 'So the big story this week is inflation.'

So I'd attempted satire before, but there's a world of difference between writing one-liners for radio and delivering a stand-up diatribe. For a start, I'd have to say it myself: no passing the script to Punt, Dennis or Toksvig and saying, 'Here are twelve jokes on the double-dip recession[2] – good luck with those.'

My wife Zoë, by now heavy with child, had time on maternity leave to join me on the road. She was rightly sceptical about my task to put the 'ha' into 'climate change' and the 'fun' into 'fundamental change in sub-Atlantic ecosystems'. I feigned confidence, all along scratching my head as to whether jokes about sustainability were really sustainable.

We toured from gig to gig, trying out green gags where possible, giving up and falling back on tried and tested material more often than not. At least I was recycling jokes. There just didn't seem to be a bedding-in ground for experimental jokes about the environment. And quite right too – if you've paid money for a comedy night, you want a laugh first and foremost, not my drawn-out opinions on why you should switch off your lights and write to your MP, though not in that order unless you're confident writing in the dark.

Wife and bump would sit at the back of the auditorium, normally quite near each other. She was spending the road trip trimming our list of baby names, since apparently Methuselah was more of a middle name, for now. I meanwhile would gauge whether to try out the new stuff, and at one such gig I asked for permission to experiment from the promoter, a stocky chap called Patrick.

'Do what you like, fella,' he replied over the beer barrels in the room behind the bar. 'They all try stuff out here. Go on long as you want.'

I just wish Patrick hadn't told that to all the acts; after a marathon four hours of show, I was to go on at nearly midnight. My wife was only six months pregnant when we came in, but was starting to be concerned about delivering right here. It was tediously late but the audience had had a great show ... till now. As the MC told them there was one act to go, a heckler cried out, 'But we've peaked!'

Never was a truer heckle spoken. I bounded on, ploughed on and dropped all the new material. Even then I had a post-show telling-off to endure from Patrick, who half-handed over my cheque but gripped it tightly as he spoke.

'Yeah you started well but I missed a lot of your punchlines cos I was chatting to my mate. You should have paused more to let us do that. You know, a lot of your jokes had words, I mean they were wordy.

[2] At least three involved taramasalata.

I can't chat to my pal and listen to you at the same time. You've got to pause more for us to chat if you want to get rebooked here.'

He finally released his grasp on my cheque and I pocketed it with a mental note to never seek that rebooking. On the journey home, I insisted to my wife that 'Patrick' be scratched from the names list.

I read, researched and tried to approach the issue of climate change from every possible comedic angle. Yet the minutiae of life kept intervening. The more I tried to talk about changing the world, the more the world seemed to wear me down.

At one provincial theatre in the Midlands, wife, bump and I drove up to the stage door and buzzed for admission to their large car park.

'We have spaces,' a brusque female voice replied through the metal box. 'But no disrespect, but you could be anyone.'

I looked at Zoë to check that this sounded as odd to her as it did to me. It did.

'Okay,' I replied to the box. 'I'm not. I'm on tonight. I'm doing the comedy show?'

'Well, you say that. Anyone could come in here and say that.'

Zoë whispered to me, 'Tell her you've got a pregnant wife.'

'I've got a wife!' I said to the box. I've never been good at passing on messages. 'Okay, all right, where else can I park?'

'St James's car park is best.'

'James, that's a nice name,' Zoë noted happily. She didn't need a nearby space, and we might see more names on road signs.

I turned back to the metallic jobsworth. 'Where's St James's?'

'You don't know where St James's is?' the box hissed.

'No,' I said, exasperated. 'I don't know if it was clear, but I'm visiting doing a show tonight for your venue. I'm not local. Could you let us park?'

A white van suddenly appeared on the other side of the gate.

'Hang on,' said the box. 'I've got to let him out.'

The gate opened, the van drove out, and we drove in. I was just putting my window back up when I heard faintly behind me: 'Right, St James's, go left out of here...' The window closed and silenced her.

Once inside, we found the nearest male employee – I didn't want to stumble upon the petty gatekeeper by mistake. He was cleaning the bar ready for the evening's audience, and had the rare mix of ponytail, nerdy glasses and nose stud. This guy was all about the facial furniture. Unfortunately he was not all about the customer service.

'Hi, I'm one of the comedians for the comedy show? This is my wife, Zoë.'

'Hi,' Zoë said. We were going to go all out on polite and friendly.

He carried on cleaning. 'So?'

'Er … is there anywhere we can put our things and just … be?'

'Café upstairs is open.'

Zoë held out her bump even more. His bespectacled eyes were only for Mr Sheen though, and he was yet to even look up.

'Right,' I tried again. 'I just wondered if there was a room for us?'

He looked up. Progress. 'A room?'

'Yes, for the comedians. Like a dressing room?'

'Of course we have dressing rooms. Big theatre, this. We've had a refurbishment, you know. Opened by the Duke of York or someone.'

'Andrew …' Zoë muttered, and wrote on a bit of paper.

'So can we use one of those?' I persisted.

He fixed me with a glare as piercing as his piercing. 'Our dressing-rooms are for performers only.' He must be related to the woman who does the gate.

I wouldn't normally have felt the need to explain the job title, but the geeky goth in front of me was pushing a few buttons. 'Comedians are performers. Aren't they … we? We do performances, like here tonight in your theatre …'

'In the studio bar,' he corrected, with a cocky push of his glasses up his nose. It struck me that his nose stud must prevent his glasses ever sliding completely off his nose, and how these piercings could be marketed with this practical purpose in mind. Maybe once I've made climate change funny, I'd put myself to that marketing plan next.

Zoë threw me a look that said: give up. We'd explore the locality to relax before show time, her thinking of names and me thinking of zingers about greenhouse gases.

I turned back to the bar cleaner, less Employee of the Month and more Employee of the Sith. 'Apart from the café upstairs, where could we find a bite to eat round here?'

He sighed and pointed out of the door we'd come in from. 'Do you know St James's?'

Zoë and I both screamed inside our heads, and left him to his Mr Sheen. He swung his ponytail smugly as we left. Because he's jobsworth it.

At this and other venues I managed to work up enough climate change material, and had soon got my act together and got my act together. It had not come naturally to me, but I knew the environmental message was a good one to get out there, and hard as it was, green issues at least provided more humour than other causes may have done. I thanked my lucky stars that the call hadn't been from a charity for orphaned landmine victims. Frankie Boyle probably has an hour on that, but I doubt the charity would like it.

The show itself ultimately had two incarnations: at a charity supporters' meeting and at Greenbelt Festival, a hub of social justice and activism. On both occasions the comedy juddered, if not flowed, but it did come. After some gradual thawing, there were rising mirth levels and carefully monitored emissions of hee, ho and hoo.

Neither may have been a barnstormer, and I'm definitely no Mark Thomas (Mark and Thomas, two more good names for the list). Bill Bailey once said that you can create jokes by starting with the laugh and working backwards, and in writing prescriptive material about the environment, I had done the polar opposite. Usually any jokes of mine that feature causes or politics haven't started with those, but with the punchline:

'When the Tories and Lib Dems formed a coalition, I liked it – blue and yellow, a bit like Ikea. Then, like Ikea, we had a rubbish cabinet that didn't last a year.'

'I've got a joke about the rising unemployment figures, but it needs work.'

'Say what you like about freedom of speech...'

In each case they're reverse-engineered, and that's generally how I work. Starting with the set-up – putting the cause before the effect – is hard, and so is dedicated activism. I just hope it helped get Operation Noah's mission of awareness out there, and that by writing this now, that this chapter does the same.

Social justice has been a burgeoning issue for the church over the last few centuries, from the formation of Methodism and The Salvation Army, to present day campaigns in many churches from the mainstream to the fringes. That's not to say non-believers don't do likewise, but these many thousands of good people have campaigned, protested and fought for what's right, with no real gain for themselves.

I can't claim to be among them. I gained on my journey: some new material for my stand-up, and a new addition to our baby names list: Noah.

* * *

Methodism – A small group of Wesleys ...

- **John Wesley**: Attendee at Oxford University, where in 1729 he formed The Holy Club with his brother Charles. Their methodical approach was mocked, but the name stuck. From there John became co-founder of Methodism, encourager of small groups, horse-riding evangelist, and keen social advocate of prison reform and against the slave trade.
- **Charles Wesley**: Co-founder of Methodism with his brother John, although Charles preferred to keep the new principles within the Church of England rather than break away. Charles was also a prolific hymn-writer, writing 'O for a Thousand Tongues', 'Love Divine, all Loves Excelling' and a little festive ditty called 'Hark! The Herald Angels Sing'.
- **Samuel Wesley**: Charles's son, John's nephew, and known as 'the English Mozart', which means he was quite good. Not that good, or Mozart would have been known as 'the Austrian Wesley'.
- **George Whitefield** (an honorary Wesley): The original open-air preacher, outstanding in his field. He'd minister to farmers and labourers on their way to work, and, fact fans, was probably the first to use the phrase 'agree to disagree', showing what a reasonable chap he was.
- **Ron Weasley**: Not a Wesley. Crucial difference.
- **Wesley Snipes**: Oh, stop it.

'Oggy oggy oggy!' I chant as we drive over the Tamar Bridge, leaving Devon and the rest of 'the mainland' behind and enter the halcyon land of Cornwall.

Zoë just stares at me.

'We are not calling the baby 'Oggy',' she insists. Which I suppose rules out the middle names of 'Oggy' and 'Oggy'.

'Come on, join in! You're Cornish by marriage now.'

'Not for long if you keep this up.'

Our tour of try-out gigs has brought the three of us – Zoë, Methuselah and myself – to the south Cornish coast. As a Cornishman, by birth if not in accent, it's a proud trip for me, and I've used the trip to throw local names at the list such as Trelawney, Petroc and Proper-Job. None are hitting the mark or pushing the right buttons, and neither's Mark, or Buttons.

With a spring Sunday morning comes a hunger for church, so a short wander leads us to a charming seafront Methodist chapel. You can't move in the West Country for Methodist chapels. All right, you can, but they have more chapels than Greggs bakers. I think.

It means a host of villages represented by chapels not churches, bonded by a strong tradition of hymn-singing and community spirit. Many Methodists abstain from alcohol, and through small groups encourage each other. It brings church fellowship right down to the bare bones of what's needed to support a community, and its mutual support is epitomised with its traditional greeting: 'How goes it with your soul?'

They don't ask that on the way in, as they opt for the English variant: 'Lovely day, isn't it?'

After a warm greeting we're ushered straight to the front row. No skulking in the back of this chapel. On looking around and seeing everyone else is going for the second row, we move back and join them. Front row for a first-timer in any church is a risk. For a start, there's no one to follow, and worse, what if everyone follows you?

There is a smattering of people here: some women who kindly notice Zoë's mid-to-large bump and give their congratulations, and some men who pretend not to notice it in case she's not pregnant and just big-wombed. One woman asks the due date, and we tell her there are two months to go. She looks relieved – mid-service delivery avoided.

Two women lead the service, and introduce themselves as Jackie and Gaynor, lay ministers. Jackie is a fortysomething Dawn French lookalike, who you can't help think was inspired to her calling by *The Vicar of Dibley*. Gaynor towers over her, and most of us, and looks like she must have bashed her head a few times on the beams in this small seaside sanctuary.

'Welcome, especially if you're a guest here,' Jackie starts, with a look not only to us but to several others around the room. They must be used to holidaymakers on the Cornish coast, and attendance here must fluctuate with the season.

There's a brief introduction by each of them, how long they've been here, how long they've been here, the names of their husbands, the pet-names of their husbands, and so on. It creates a friendly atmosphere, and the service seems to reflect this informal nature. There are no dog-collars here, no stained glass, and the cross at the front of the church is simple, wooden, and propped up on a shelf. There is no pomp in this ceremony.

Gaynor ducks under a beam and steps forward. 'We're very much hoping to be joined later by Joseph, who many of you will know.'

The dozen or so regulars make noises of pleasant surprise, and there's clearly a very warm feeling towards Joseph, whoever he may be.

'He's playing the piano up at St Andrew's on the hill, then with a bit of luck and the wind behind him, he'll be cycling down to join us to play the organ by the end of the service.'

'Cycling!' one of the congregants says to her neighbour, among the other impressed sounds we hear in the church. Clearly Joseph was not one for cycling normally.

'So that will be lovely,' Gaynor concludes.

Jackie's turn: 'So first we're going to sing a familiar song, we hope you'll know it, number 68 in your books, "O God our Help in Ages Past".'

There's a rustling of books that I've not heard for many years in a church. It's a reassuring sound from my youth, pre-PowerPoint. This trip truly is a homecoming.

In my younger days though they'd never have had what we see before us now: a CD-playing boom box that Gaynor is struggling with. She skips forward to the correct track (confusingly it's not track 68, like in our books), and we all guess when to come in for a rendition of Charles Wesley's classic hymn. While this Joseph fellow plays piano for the Anglicans up the hill, we're left with a CD, that's starting to skip.

The thought occurs to me that I can't paint a picture of this Joseph. Is he eight or eighty? He's probably nowhere in between; the good will from the locals and the astonishment that he's cycling means that he must either be impressively young to play piano and ride a bike between churches, or a spritely old gent. My mind isn't made up, and I sit on the fence, as I'm sure young Joseph did swinging his feet seventy odd years back, or last Saturday. One or the other.

The service continues warmly, uncontroversially and traditionally. The Methodist way may not have the formal structure of Catholics or high Anglicans, but it does have its gentle traditions. Not for this church the drum kits and projector screens of the modern age. Here we find a simple, stripped-down service of song, prayer and preaching. It's a chance for us to simply give thanks, once again, that my medical ridiculousness has been overcome to give us lovely Theo the Foetus.

There is no Holy Communion today – it's rarer among Methodists, although does occur. The sung worship is not overly showy or elaborate, and there are none of the freeform elements that some churches encourage. Many churches have more of an open floor for prayer or prophecy, or the worship leader has licence to go off-piste. Here the worship is so fixed, it's on CD.

Of course this is just for today, while we're waiting for Joseph's musical accompaniment. But there is a general air that we have put our trust in the ministers to guide us through this service; the authority is placed in their hands.

As Jackie gives the Bible reading, and hands over to Gaynor for the sermon, I'm left realising what a credit these women are to the church. They cast light on the insanity of the long wait in the neighbouring C of E for women bishops. I have every confidence that in centuries from now, they'll look back at church history in disbelief that it was left solely in the hands of men for so long. I'm sure the more turbulent parts of Christianity's past, from crusades to cover-ups, would have been a very different story if women had had a bit more say.

'It's time for our last song,' says Jackie with a frown. 'And there's no Joseph.'

The congregation join in a group frown, as do Zoë and I. We're upset too. We'll never get to meet the old man/young boy. Joseph is Godot.

A CD is found, and after a minute's pause to discover which track number relates to which number in the book, we join in with Hymn Number 143/Track 6, 'Love Divine, all Loves Excelling'.

We're getting all the hearty Charles Wesley classics today. I wouldn't be surprised if we followed it with 'Hark! The Herald Angels Sing', even though it is April.

As the service ends, congregants lean from row to row and catch up. Zoë and I appraise the pleasant, uncomplicated service with a simple: 'Very nice.'

'Yes, very nice,' she replies.

An uncluttered review of an uncluttered service. Ministering hasn't needed to change much here since John Wesley preached in fields and to farmers as they laboured. Still today, Jackie and Gaynor bring straightforward services with a strong community feel. Methodism was in many ways aimed at the working class who felt unwelcomed by the mainline church. This small chapel at the heart of the village has once again had that unpretentious broad appeal for those who want a place to sing, pray and hear preaching.

It's church at street level, where elements of the service live or die not by whether certain buttons are pressed on a computer, but whether the organist can cycle down the hill in time.

'The CD player was an interesting touch.'

'Yes. Shame we didn't hear Joseph's organ playing. I suppose they share a musician between the churches.'

'Mmm,' I say. My eyes glaze and Zoë's eyes roll because she knows the look – I've thought of a joke. 'They need their own worship leader perhaps. A rhythm Methodist.'

Zoë glares, as do others. A time and a place, Paul.

Her glare is stopped short as we hear the front door burst open. We quickly turn. Could this, in the nick of time, be Joseph?

A sixty-year-old man enters puffing. It has to be ...

'Joseph?' exclaims Gaynor.

... It is!

The wheezing latecomer takes a moment, then speaks: 'He's not going to make it.'

... It isn't.

'St Andrew's overran, and then his bike had a puncture.'

The regulars mumble regretfully: 'Poor Joseph ... A puncture of all things ...'

He sits and pants, and Zoë turns to me. 'So is that Joseph's dad, or ... How old do you think Joseph is?'

'Exactly!' I cry. 'Is he a boy? Is he a pensioner?'

Gaynor rushes past to reassure the newsbearer that we've finished anyway, and she nearly smacks into a low beam as she goes. A swift limbo shows that she knows the layout of this chapel well.

Jackie saunters past us, and I collar her with a question: 'Excuse me, can I just ask? This 'Joseph'...'

'No!' Zoë says, putting her hand between us like she's stopping a fight. 'I don't want to know.'

Jackie smiles and moves on.

'Best we don't find out,' Zoë says to me. 'Well it just works if he's young or old.'

I agree. Some names – Maisie, Boo-boo, Elmo – sound great for kids but I can't imagine them aged eighty. Others – Doris, Frank, Methuselah – are probably best only adopted when you retire. 'Joseph' works for both, and works for both of us.

We resolve that if it's a boy, we'll call him Joseph.

13

Up Above the Streets and Houses

Handling Hot Potatoes

It was a boy, so we called him Joseph.

He was and is, of course, a delight, with occasional elements of screaminess. The whole experience was a total whirlwind. We didn't sleep for the excitement before the birth, and we didn't sleep a huge amount afterwards.

I became a recluse for a few weeks, knee-deep in a world of nappies, sleeplessness and 3 a.m. trips to the 24-hour Tesco for new nappies – zombie-like, yet somehow enjoying the trip out.

Gigs were hard work for a while as I operated on Red Bull and good will. I took less work on and tried not to drive as far, although inevitably just a few less gigs than normal does affect your stage performance.

I had a comedy festival, which necessitated me doing as many guest spots as possible at as many venues as possible, to plug my own solo show. I'd do five minute spots, little advertisements for my hour-long show, and end each set with the venue and time of my solo show.

It always sounds awkward – comedy is for telling it like it is, not flogging your wares. I've heard numerous comics banging out anti-consumerist, anti-individualist rants, then wrapping up by plugging a book or DVD they're selling at the back for a fiver. To survive, the stand-up comic needs to be capitalist but sound anti-capitalist. To see my latest range of anti-capitalist merchandise, visit www.paulkerensa.com.

On one such day I managed seven gigs, which was almost too many, running from venue to venue, doing callbacks to jokes that I'd told to previous audiences. Two poor lads saw me at noon and again at midnight across town, thanks to their bad luck. They started heckling my punchlines, fresh in their heads because they'd only heard them a few hours before. By that point I was hoarse, tired, and mistakenly aiming putdowns at people from three gigs ago.

Guest spot number six was a gig I'd booked myself when passing the venue. I'd seen them advertising a charity comedy show, with names on the bill that were not vastly up the pecking order from me. I almost felt entitled to a gig there.

Thanks to guest spot number five running late, I arrived at this pub to hear the show in full swing. The landlord was outside smoking as he yelled, 'Where've you been?! You're due on!'

'I'm so sorry,' I said. 'Who's on now?'

'Nigel, local performance poet. Have you seen him? Every two lines, he takes off a layer of clothing. Ends up stark naked. He's here every year. Crowd loves him.'

Wow, I thought. My whimsy about parenthood and geekery might be a bit of a comedown after that.

The landlord continued, 'We'll have an interval after you, cos it's the Scottish Gay Men's Chorus and they need time to set up.' Quite a line-up they've got here.

Inside the venue I heard an almighty cheer, which indicated that Nigel had reached his big finish. The compère briefly took the stage to announce my name, and I ran in, leapt onstage, and started my set. At my feet, a naked Nigel picked up his clothes.

'Scuse the exhaustion, we've got one of those … what do you call them? … Babies!' I began.

No cheer. Never mind, some audiences don't. I haven't taken off any clothes, so perhaps they cheer here at different things. I tried to claw a response from them:

'Who here's got kids?'

No one, apparently. They say talk about what you know, and right now, this was all I knew. This was an all-male audience, but surely it doesn't take a woman to reply. Some of the men were a bit older, and I thought must be at grandparent level by now. Maybe they just didn't like me and didn't want to join in. I tried to win it back by getting feisty:

'Are we all barren?!'

Nothing. Not even an ooh. Just the slow hum of conversation beginning. That's the worst thing to hear as a comedian. Heckling's better than general chat – far better.

And then the penny, like Nigel's trousers, dropped. A voice in my head did a *Through The Keyhole*-style recap as Lloyd Grossman: 'Who would drink in a bar like this? Let's look at the evidence: Nigel the stripping poet. The Scottish Gay Men's Chorus. Every comedian but me being gay or lesbian. The all-male audience. The annual fundraiser for a local Aids charity. The rainbow flags outside. David, it's over to you.'

All were clues, you might say. I'd say to you that I am clearly so free of prejudice and bias that I don't see things that others might. Yes, it was a tricky performance once I'd realised this was an all-gay gig, and I probably wouldn't have begun as I did had I known. But I did my time, and closed with the mandatory: 'I'm in The George function room at 8 p.m. Come along! No need for babysitters.' Finally, they laughed.

A few weeks later and I was back at my usual pace of life on the road, stopping at hotels and spare rooms. I treated myself to nicer accommodation, which was needless since I was so tired most of the time that I'd sleep for twelve hours straight in a bus shelter if necessary.

There's been a sliding scale over the years of what I'll plump for. When I started out in my early twenties, I'd stay on floors. Once it wasn't even a living-room floor, but a kitchen floor, being woken up at 3 a.m. by the promoter's wife home from nightshift defrosting some bread. It wasn't the sound of the toaster that woke me, but the freezer door being slammed into my head.

I outgrew floors and insisted on sofas, which again was fine until the tenant's flatmates would wake me to play Xbox on the living-room telly. Then I became all prima donna and would ask for a spare room. At this rate I soon won't stay anywhere without a personal jacuzzi, turn-down service and Corby trouser press next to a little kettle.

For now a popular stop-off is of course with friends, and one old friend – and vicar – had uttered those three silly words to me: 'Stay any time.'

The week of the gig, I texted him to check his address. I thought I could probably find it; I knew the village he was in, so figured I'd just head there, find the big pointy building, and knock on the vicarage next door.

'Apartment 8a, Ironworks Street' came the reply, along with a city centre postcode. An urban church, I thought – maybe he was now a town centre chaplain. I'd heard of these yet never seen them. I imagine they're like an ecclesiastical high-street ninja. I love the idea of clergy mixing with town shoppers incognito, then bursting out with a quick prayer while you're queuing in M&S: 'Please God let them have this in an 18 for this woman ... Sorry, 16, my mistake.'

I knew Luke had a nice little Church of England parish, with, I had always presumed, a charming rectory and a Sunday school teacher called Alex. They'd eventually marry in a lovely ceremony attended by the whole community, with school kids dancing around the maypole. That's always been my impression anyway. Ironworks Street slightly shook up that world. Perhaps, I thought, he doesn't live in a village called Dibley in a county called Midsomer.

'Yes,' he said when I double-checked.'I *was* in the vicarage. That was before ... Well there have been a few changes.'

Luke had come out. The Sunday school teacher myth was on hold, although Alex could be Alexander. This might have surprised me, but as we know from the gay bar gig, my gaydar is so bad that if it were real radar, no airport would employ me. Closet doors could be swinging open all around me, and all I'd notice was a slight draught, thinking it's the window. I'm the sort of person who'd meet Louie Spence and his female assistant and ask how long they'd been married.

I arrived in Ironworks Street and Luke explained more.

'I was expecting a bit of a showdown with the bishop,' Luke told me over a cup of tea.'I was hoping for instant martyr status. Actually he was pretty okay about it. Even sent me a very nice congratulations card.'

The new Luke looked just like the old Luke. There was no tight-fitting T-shirt, and I probably had more pink shirts than he did. We just picked up where we left off, except now in a fashionable apartment block rather than a country vicarage.

Luke related that many of his neighbours were also gay, but more through coincidence than design – this wasn't specifically the 'gay district', just that these flats were quite nice, and only affordable by DINKYs (Double Income No Kids Yet). But even the DINKYs often move out to suburban semi-detacheds, using their 'DI' to get a garden for when they have 'K' later. That leaves these pricey metropolitan flats for not so much DINKYs, as DINKs.

'There is a big gay scene in this city,' Luke said, adding, 'But it's not for me. We prefer the pub down the road. Good ales, good pub quiz.'

The 'we' is Luke and his civil partner John. Gay priesthood *and* gay marriage – two ecclesiastical hot potatoes rolled together into a giant plate of mash, that a lot of people don't know how to digest. As for me, I've always thought the major awkwardness of a same-gender wedding is the usher greeting attendees asking, 'Is it groom's side or groom's side?' … before seating you anywhere.

At the time of writing, marriage is still the preserve of Adam and Eve, not Adam and Steve, nor indeed Madam and Eve. But this may soon change. The political atmosphere is moving towards it: civil partnership is not enough for many, and true equality means that traditional marriage needs to be redefined. If it passes, then individual churches may or may not be forced to conduct same-sex weddings. That said, B&B owners have been forced to accommodate same-sex couples against their will, so whether the organised church can hold out in the courts longer than the B&B industry, remains to be seen.

'So are you ex-Anglican?' I asked Luke, still trying to work out where he now fitted in church life.

'I'm ex-parish, still Anglican. Ish.'

He'd become a prison chaplain, employed by the Home Office, and was therefore under their equal opportunities protections. I sensed he'd had his metaphorical bag packed and was ready to leave the C of E for good, from parish to pariah. Then the bishop was a bit more accepting than expected, so he took a sideways step into prison ministry.

Luke clarified, 'My services in prison are Anglican. I'm still licensed by the diocese.'

Luke had done an unusual thing in even telling his bishop – many don't. And his bishop was gracious in response – some aren't.

The Church and Homosexuality

With more stances than a Gap catalogue model, here's a simplified opinion spectrum (or rainbow):

> 'Do not adopt the customs of the people who live there.'
> – Leviticus 20:23

RED: … in the face. These placard-wielding extremists have closet doors and minds that are nailed shut. Their numbers are thankfully minimal, and Louis Theroux has them on speed-dial.

'Neither fornicators, nor idolaters, nor adulterers, nor homosexuals, nor sodomites, nor thieves, nor covetous, nor drunkards, nor revilers, nor extortioners will inherit the kingdom of God. And such were some of you. But you were washed ...' – *I Corinthians 6:9-11*

ORANGE: The future's bright, the future's straight, if you 'pray away the gay', 'convert the flirt', 'minister to the sinister', and so on. If the far-far-right go large with their beliefs to a placard-sized A0, the far-righters keep theirs to a handy A5 pamphlet size. You might hear of people being 'ex-gay' or 'post-gay', though I doubt that my friend Luke thinks of himself as 'ex-straight'. Besides, I can't hear 'ex-gay' without thinking of Monty Python's parrot sketch: 'This man is no more a homosexual, he has ceased to be attracted to men, he's no longer a friend of Dorothy and he's joined the heterosexuals ... This, is an ex-gay.'

'Love the sinner, hate the sin.' – *Gandhi*

YELLOW: The only association I can find with 'yellow' is that this is quite middle-of-the-road, and, er, so are Coldplay. And they had a hit with 'Yellow'. Ahem ...

Gandhi's quote has been adopted by many in the church, and is often misattributed to the Bible. Perhaps the biblical quote best seen with it is: *'He who is without sin among you, let him be the first to throw a stone.'* – *John 8:7.*

I don't know that it's up to me to hate anyone else's sin. God can, and I'm sure will, loathe a good deal of the sins we commit. I don't care to number mine: there's going to be a lot. So how about, 'Love the sinner, let God judge the sin'? Not as catchy, but just a thought. I'm not a preacher or theologian though, so what do I know ... I'm just a bloke who doesn't like hating things (except maybe Coldplay).

– 'a Bible quote of everything the gospels say directly about homosexuality.'

GREEN: Jesus said nothing about it, nor did any Jewish prophet. Paul's letters refers to it, where it's listed alongside lying, cheating and adultery, so it's a sin, but one of many, and we're all guilty. So the centrist attitude is largely a shrug of the shoulders. There are no pamphlets or placards (hooray – think of the trees, hence this is 'green'), and no concerted efforts to pray away so much as a fondness for Wham CDs.

There's an acknowledgement of the Bible's various negative comments on homosexuality, which cannot be ignored, but the focus is elsewhere – in a world of poverty and myriad secular challenges for the church, the centre ground tries not to get bogged down in who fancies who in their congregation. Growing up as I did in Dibley, Midsomer, we didn't have homosexuality in our church, at least not that I noticed during the service (but then I sat quite near the front).

'This is the will of God, your sanctification; that you abstain from sexual immorality.' – I Thessalonians 4:3

BLUE: Time to get blue: let's talk about sex. More liberally, church leadership may now include gay people in church leadership, but on the condition of their celibacy. The Church of England allows gay people to be priests, but biblical teaching on sex outside marriage means they must abstain. Yet if gay people want to marry, the church says they can't. It's a vicious circle (but enough about wedding rings).

'Accept one another, then, just as Christ accepted you, in order to bring praise to God.' – Romans 15:7

INDIGO: ... In yer go, into church, everybody. Gay, straight, tall, short, all welcome, all able to participate in sacraments, be ordained and marry.

This school of thought doesn't think 'tolerance' goes far enough. Bad smells are tolerated. Someone eating a kebab next to you on the train is tolerated (or more often not). People should be welcomed and made to feel part of the community. Saying to a gay couple, 'You're welcome in our church, because that loving committed relationship you've got, it's merely on a par with lying and cheating ...' may not be as welcoming as it could be.

There is a paradox – parts of the Bible do condemn homosexuality. Yet we need to be a loving church. The world is too full of bigger problems than this. Maybe we should accept that, like why anyone would want a kebab on the morning commuter train, it's just a sweet mystery of life.

'Some are incapable of marriage because they were born so ... there are others who have renounced marriage for the sake of the kingdom of Heaven. Let those accept it who can.' – Matthew 19:11-12

VIOLET: At the end of the rainbow, there's our final strand of thinking: those churches that actively affirm the LGBT[1] community and encourage them in, or meet them on the street. Jesus spoke widely of love, discipleship and faithfulness, and idea of a 'civil partnership at Cana' just wasn't in the culture at the time.

'Christians Together at Pride' marched in London's Pride parade, while placards were waved at the sidelines by other Christians back in red zone of the opinion spectrum. When they'd finished processing alongside non-Christian LGBTers, there was a service for Pride marchers at Bloomsbury Central Baptist Church.

Luke told me of a similar venture. 'There's a church in Liverpool, St Bride's, with a regular gay-friendly service. Every month they have a service called Open Table, for and by the LGBT community. In terms of liturgy it's the straightest thing they do. As for Paul's writings, he doesn't even mention lesbians, bisexuals, or transgendered people, and it looks like his concern was for exploitative encounters. What he would make of loving same-sex relationships remains a mystery. We might as well ask Julius Caesar to draw a penguin.'

While churches the world over decide which colour they're painting themselves, Christianity is tarnished. In a recent survey, when asked for words associated with Christians, Americans

[1] Lesbian, Gay, Bisexual, or Transgender. For the first time in this book, a useful footnote.

---

came up not with words like 'loving' and 'caring', but 'homophobic' and 'bigoted'. Christians I know are helping the poor, feeding the hungry, and generally 'being nice'. So thanks to our disunity about this one issue, we're being massively misrepresented. Perhaps it's time that whatever colour we are, we all got well over the rainbow, friend of Dorothy or not.

'The truth is, that outside of churches, no one is that interested,' Luke told me. 'It's no longer a secret at work. As chaplain I'm not even "the only gay in prison" – again, martyrdom denied. So bizarrely, I've found freedom in prison.'

'Sounds like there's a bit of a love/hate relationship with the C of E?' I asked.

'Quakers,' Luke said. 'If I had my time again, with a level playing field, I'd be a Quaker.'

'Any reason?' I was trying to cover my ignorance – I knew little of the Quakers. I knew they had something to do with cereal, but I couldn't remember which one. I think it was Shreddies.

'You ever been to a Friends Meeting?' Luke asked.

'I watched season one to four pretty much back to back with a couple of mates. I was Chandler, they fought over who was Joey and Ross.'

'Friends, Quakers, same people,' he clarified. 'Their way of worship, got to be the most radical I've ever encountered.' Bold words, especially for one who's gone from village vicar to LGBT-themed service via Heaven (the nightclub). 'And obviously they have a hugely important history in this country. Not least prison reform.'

'Of course,' I said. 'Goes without saying.' I made a mental note to have a date with Wikipedia later.

'They got them privacy in prison. Prisoners learning a trade – that comes from early Quakers. Anti-slavery campaigners and all. They've done a good lot.'

I resolved to look into the Quakers; they sound like historical good eggs. It's good to remember that social justice isn't a new concept in UK Christianity. Christians don't leave people behind, or at least haven't, till now.

14

Friends and Other Sitcoms

Querying with Quakers

I'd landed a part in a sitcom. In America this would be the route to stardom.[1] For our Atlantically-challenged cousins, the route is: comedy circuit, comedy circuit, comedy circuit, sitcom role, bad comedy film, good comedy film, host Oscars. Here in the UK it's more: open mic circuit, pro circuit, sitcom part/panel show appearance, advert, bad comedy film, pro circuit, open mic circuit, death. I'm moving to America.

But in the meantime, Mr Kerensa, we're ready for your close-up.

I was so excited! I'd spent years working up to this. I'd done my time behind the scenes: writing, writing more, fetching coffee (all right, only for myself, while writing). I'd only acted on camera in front of the window at Currys Digital.

I needed this. Gone were the days of spending all my earnings on DVDs. Since becoming a parent, I couldn't afford them and wouldn't find time to watch them if I did. There was that transitional month when I bought five DVDs, realised I'd never watch them and they've sat there on the shelf ever since. It means I can time the exact moment that my carefree life ended: Old Paul ceased to be when *The Dark Knight* was released. (I'm told it's a good film – I've yet to get the chance to find out.)

That's not to say that I hadn't been frugal in my bachelor days, but I think it's fair to say I was 'differently frugal'. I'd happily blow money on wine, women and song,[2] while scrimping on essentials like food. One day I found myself at home eating a Victoria sponge cake for lunch, just

[1] The importance of punctuation. When I first wrote that, it read, 'I landed a part in a sitcom, in America.' Which would have been a much bigger deal.
[2] Smirnoff Ice, dating attempts and karaoke.

because at 99p it was cheaper than a sandwich. I didn't even slice it – I just ate it like a burger. I'd have got away with it had my flatmate not walked in and queried my serving suggestion and dietary choice, ignoring my bleatings that jam is fruit.

Sitcom big-time was what I needed to kick start the toddler's university fund, the very second I'd filled the tax bill fund and paid off the debt from 2009's holiday fund. Since starting out as a comedian, I'd seen up-and-comers up and go. Open spots overtook. I've introduced Jack Whitehall as an open spot, compèred Sarah Millican at a new act competition, and attempted to follow Michael McIntyre.[3] So this could be my time. Stardom was calling and I had to answer, or knowing me I'd let it go to voicemail because I didn't recognise the number.

I had a rare glimpse of the celebrity lifestyle years back, when flatmate Danny blagged us tickets to a show by one of his magician friends, Derren Brown.[4] The event would combine two of my favourite things: magic and freebies. It would be the press night, so we'd be in the same audience as celebs like Jonathan Ross, as well as normal people like Paul Ross.

I've always been a fan of 'doubling up' as a comic, so I used the trip to the big smoke to visit my accountant. He had forms for me to sign, and my fifteen pound rail fare would save him the 42p stamp. So I donned my only suit, because I think you're meant to do that for accountants. It was one of those halfway posh outfits, where a top designer stoops to doing a range for M&S. One that says, 'The person who made this normally charges a grand a suit, so this one's only a hundred pounds because it's a collection of offcuts glued together.'

Accountant and I pored over some figures for an hour, before concluding I had approximately no money. Then he billed me for that hour's work, so I now had less than no money.

'Back home now?' he asked chirpily, reclining in his better-suit-than-mine.

'No,' I replied. 'Off to a top West-End show. First night.'

'Can you afford that? Let me re-show you the figures ...'

'Not if it eats into a second hour,' I added hastily. 'Anyway the tickets were free.'

I gathered any paperwork I needed, including the receipt for the suit,

[3] Not as in 'home'.
[4] Clang.

which would be going back next week based on today's findings.

I headed to the West End, but the badly-lit number-crunching had come at a cost. My new contact lenses – hard, evil lenses – had not reacted well to staring at digits, particularly the red ones. I nearly swung via Superdrug for some eye drops, till I spotted Poundland over the road and swung via there instead. Big pound shops have a pharmacy section – a good tip for the unhealthy and unwealthy. The budget eye drops didn't help alas, though the 99p Victoria sponge I bought for dinner at least brightened my spirits, and there was not a trace of jam on my nice suit.

As I approached the theatre for my first 'first night', my corneas were weeping as they pressed against the fierce contact lenses, and even the murky autumnal half-light was blinding me. Passers-by thought I was upset. The truth was, I was just in pain. I remembered I had sunglasses in my jacket pocket from the last time I'd worn the suit – a wedding, on a brighter day. I donned them, and rounded the corner to the impressive Cambridge Theatre. Through my sunglasses and teary eyes I saw the giant Derren Brown poster, and a ton of press photographers flanking the main entrance.

A soap star walked in, and the cameras snapped. Half a dozen non-famous people entered and the photographers lowered their cameras to the floor. How demeaning. I hurried in behind the muggles, not wanting to follow a celeb myself and experience the photographers' rejection.

Yet as soon as I got near them, all the cameras went up again, to me. There was no one else around, but I heard click after click. I had a fly's eye of lenses pointing at me from both sides as I walked up the red carpet.

I knew in an instant that it was all a mistake. They'd seen a sharp-suited chap with sunglasses on at dusk, and thought, 'Well, he has to be famous.' They'd take all the snaps they could now, then work out later that I was actually a nobody. I was a fraud, but a fraud enjoying the moment.

'Over here! Over here!' the mob screamed. They wanted poses.

I turned and gave them a few, when one photographer spoke out. I knew in an instant I'd been rumbled: the Emperor wasn't wearing new clothes after all.

'No, wait. Look at his carrier bag.'

As the cameras all drooped, so did my eyes, to see that yes, I was indeed clutching a bag from Poundland. My fifteen seconds of fame was over …

… Till now. With my big sitcom part around the corner, I made sure my lines were learnt and my call-time checked. Everything was ready for my TV acting debut, but I still had a Sunday morning free and a curiosity about the Quakers. I'd wanted to give them a try since my chaplain friend recommended them, so ahead of the sitcom appearance, I went to meet some new Friends.

* * *

I enter a small semi-detached house, where I find a handful of strangers. Over the road is a large traditional gothic church, with dozens of suited people rushing in. But today that's not for me.

Our building is plain and single storey, but there's no ignoring the large sign outside: 'Friends Meeting House: All welcome'. It starts with 'Friends', it ends with 'welcome'. That's nice, isn't it?

The hallway greeting is true to the sign, and a kind elderly woman looks at me with an 'Ooh!' I must be their first newbie for a while.

'You're new here. Have you been to a Quaker meeting before?'

I admit not, but that I have Wikipedia'd them. She breathes a sigh of relief yet still recaps the key points that any visitor should know, i.e. that it's largely silent, and that there's no minister. We all sit anywhere we want.

'Many new people find the silence a bit unbearable,' she confides. 'If you need to leave, that's okay.'

I imagine previous first-timers lasting five minutes then running into the street screaming, desperately breaking into cars and turning the radios on loud just to hear some noise. I think I'll be okay. If she thinks I'm not used to silence, she's never been to one of my gigs.

She gestures me through a door, telling me, 'A few of them are in. That means we've started.'

I walk in, and she's right – here the meeting begins 'when two or three are gathered', as Matthew 18:20 decrees. And here are the two or three: a goateed sixty-something reading a Bible in the corner, a middle-aged man deep in thought with the classic fingers-on-chin-and-index-finger-up-the-cheek pose to prove it everyone, and an older chap reading the Bible on his iPad. He's the oldest person I've ever seen comfortably using a tablet, at least of the non-paracetamol variety.

So the atmosphere is a nice mix of tradition and the cutting-edge. I sense that I'm in a meeting steeped in history, yet due to the simplicity of the set-up, it doesn't feel dated, and an iPad fits in quite comfortably here. The simple layout is a square of chairs around the walls, with a central circle in the middle around a table. There is no altar, no nave, no cross; this is no church. There is a piano, which surprises me, for a fellowship that is known for its silence and lack of sung worship.

Quaker worship is different – today we'll be worshipping the same God that the Anglicans over the road are, but while they are invited to now sing 'How Great Thou Art', omitting verse four, we'll be invited to omit all verses, of all hymns. We'll worship as a collective in a time of quiet waiting. The hope is to hear God's still small voice of calm, as these Friends aim to emulate the early Christians.

That is not to say no one will speak aloud. If someone feels moved by the Holy Spirit to speak up, then they can. God leads this service. I've read that some weeks, no one says anything but sometimes you can't shut them up (by which I mean three people might speak for a minute each – it's all relative). Today, I have no idea which it will be.

I sit with the others in peace and wait upon God. Then thoughts enter my brain – shopping lists, things I meant to set the video for, do we call it a video nowadays, because it's not a video is it, it's meant to be called a DVR, but that hasn't caught on, has it? ...

I've become distracted pretty quickly. This is my problem in times of prayer. When at my regular church, and Marjorie leads the prayers saying, 'We will now leave a moment of silence for you to offer your own prayers,' that's when my brain instantly pipes up with eighteen different distractions that have been just waiting to burst out. By the time I've dismissed them all, mentally minimising them to the taskbar, the prayers are over and we're onto the church notices. Perhaps here with the Quakers, an hour of silence is what I need to get past my brain's interruptions and actually get conversing with the Creator. I can afford to acknowledge my mind's distractions, move past them, and maybe get to some quality G-time before the end of the hour.

I decide it starts now. No distractions. Time to get my pray on, because any moment, one of my three co-attendees could be moved to speak. I wonder how long before someone speaks. A minute? Ten minutes? Fifty-nine minutes? Perhaps no one will say anything till the very end, when one of the Friends will stand suddenly and say, 'Nuff said,' before moonwalking out of the meeting house.

First words uttered at 10.53 a.m. – that's the bet I make with myself. Is it wrong to use prayer time to make fake bets in your head? Undoubtedly. I mentally confess that sin, then carry on doing it.

I remember a wedding reception when our table had a pound sweepstake on the length of the speeches. One by one, everyone's guesses came and went, till it was just two people left: my dad and me. I felt a bit guilty clock-watching while the best man gave Aunt Madge's apologies for absence, but the look in my dad's eyes became fiercely competitive, so as time went on I willed the speaker to start wrapping up. If he stopped talking in the next minute, I'd win the eight pounds; if he had any more apologies or anecdotes, my dad got the lot, and more importantly, braggers' rights.

'… So a big thank you to all the ushers. Let's now charge our glasses for …'

Applause suddenly broke out.

'Oh you're right,' added the best man. 'Clap the ushers.'

My dad grinned – he had started the applause. He looked at me and gestured to his watch. He was going to win, and he was quite prepared to artificially get some applause going to drag these speeches out.

The best man tried again to finish. 'So let's now charge our glasses …'

'What about the waitresses?!' my dad heckled.

'Oh, oh yes, they've been good too. Thank you waitresses. So charge your …'

My dad started clapping again, and once more the whole room joined in, amid mumbles of people saying things like, 'Yes the waitresses are doing a great job,' or, 'Why are we clapping the waitresses?'

Dad continued, 'And the bride's auntie. She folded napkins.'

'Yes, well we have to draw the line somewhere,' the best man replied, champagne flute in mid-toast.

'Hey!' yelled the bride's auntie across the room.

The assembled mass started to inspect the origami of their napkins, and the best man turned to my dad. 'Anyone else I've left out?'

My dad, the only one in the room laughing, slowed his guffaw, checked his watch and reported back, 'No, that's fine, thank you.'

As glasses were finally charged, toasts were given and the speeches brought to a close, my dad gathered up his eight pounds and a wrathful glare from me as a bonus. You can't just hijack someone's wedding speeches to win a bet. It's wrong, especially if I lose.

All of this takes three seconds to race through my head as another Quaker joins the meeting. I chastise myself for my 10.53 a.m. prediction, and embrace the silence once more.

'Hi there,' the latest arrival whispers to me.

Does he not know the rules? I've only been here five minutes but even I know more than him.

'I'm the clerk of the meeting,' he continues in hushed tones. 'I hear it's your first time at a Quaker meeting?'

Is this a test? Am I meant to reply? I thought we were under exam conditions? No talking, no looking at each other's Bibles, no flicking rulers at the legs of anyone wearing short trousers.

I decide to reply quietly. 'Yes. I'm Paul. Thanks for having me.'

'Oh you're most welcome, Paul.' He introduces himself. 'Dave. Do you know that the meeting is mostly conducted in silence?'

Do *you* know, I think. I nod.

'Here're a couple of books – some people like to read for a bit.'

I wonder what he's going to give me – I hear *The Hunger Games* is an interesting yarn, or there's a couple of good uns on Richard & Judy's Book Club. I remember where I am, and so quite rightly he hands me a Bible, and a book titled *Quaker Faith & Practice*.

'Any other questions?' he asks. Others look up though as if we're the naughty kids in a library. He may be the clerk but he's clearly 'the chatty one'. He doesn't wait for me to reply. 'See you after.' And he crosses the room looking sheepish.

A further six or seven enter the room and choose seats – these Quakers are a little late, but they've probably been having their porridge. Each sits anywhere – there is no front or back, as in a regular church. So it does seem a little like a psychological exercise: 'who will sit where'. Will you head right up to the flowers for a good whiff? Or hide in the corner? One tries three seats before settling.

Now more people have joined us, the silence takes on a presence of its own. Is this God? The Spirit? Or some sense of the combined focus of a roomful of worshippers?

I pick up the second book Dave gave me. It's a mighty tome: a regularly-updated, country-specific manual for Quaker living, handily broken-down into bitesize chunks. The first part is called 'Advices &

Queries'. I thought that was a *Guardian* column where people email in questions like, 'How long *is* a piece of string?' or, 'Why *do* birds suddenly appear every time you are near?' But no, these 'queries' are open-ended questions, designed for reflections, exercises and general spiritual challenges. It reads as practical guidance for living good lives, and speaks beyond just faith. Issues such as community, tolerance, openness and diligence all come up frequently. My image of a Quaker was pretty old-fashioned and twee, but now I see that's far from the truth: their book indicates they're progressive and very keen to engage with the modern world, and with other beliefs.

Well into the meeting half are reading their books or iPads, with the other half in meditative prayer. Some eyes are closed, some are open and looking towards the autumn sunshine beaming in. Bible open, I try to focus my mind on higher things. The shopping list, the order of best actors to play *Doctor Who* – all briefly occur to me, because they shouldn't, and I put them to one side.

My friend Luke was right; it does feel radical. I'm taking my time to get into it, yes, but all of the thoughts above manage to flick through my head in just a few seconds. For the next fifty minutes, I pray well, and hard, and I feel a strong power communally in the room, unsung and unspoken. The combined silence and spiritual focus here seems like more than the sum of its parts.

After nearly an hour of silence, someone suddenly speaks. It shatters the silence, even though it's a frail soft voice.

'I was just thinking,' she bursts out timidly, then stands, 'that we should remember Advices & Queries number 1.05.' She then reads it aloud. It consists of an advice – to take time to learn about the experience of others – followed by some queries – What can we impart back? Should we consider the value of doubt and questioning more? She ends by adding in a beautifully meek voice: 'I just thought that should be something we all should consider.'

She sits, and each listener demonstrates thought and reflection: some of us nod, some return to putting fingers on chin pensively. I wonder if she's dwelling on learning about others because I'm here – am I the first newbie in a while?

A minute goes by. Then Dave the clerk stands in response.

'I'd like to echo Lily's words. And also add that we should take time to listen to our own experiences too.'

He sits. We mull on his words. Some return to their Bibles. iPad man returns to whatever game he's playing. I return to prayer.

The next movement in the room is ten minutes later, when Dave the clerk leans over to his nearest neighbour and shakes his hand. We all take the cue and shake hands with others near us, and although no one speaks, the silence changes – it's no longer a holy stillness, but a quiet rustling and readjustment of sitting positions. A few people cough, like they've been saving them up, and I suddenly realise – and am thankful – that through the hour of stillness, there were no stomach-rumblings, mini-burps or windypops. Unlike some theatre audiences, this gathering knows how to be properly noiseless.

Two young children enter the room with a helper – this is presumably the Sunday school equivalent – and the clerk stands and addresses the room in a more informal manner.

'Well, good morning to you all.' A quiet 'good morning' is mumbled. 'And a particular welcome to Paul. Nice to have you along.'

I nod a thanks. Notices follow: a garden lunch, a plea for charity volunteers, and an announcement of the evening's service (where I imagine the silence is livelier and more aimed at young people).

Tea follows, and Dave makes his way back over to me. I tell him how much I've enjoyed the session – and I thoroughly have. I think the silence may drive me potty if I came every week, but it was so nice to have space, and have a time of worship that is unplanned yet far from unfocused. In a regular service, when the reading gives way to prayers, and the prayers give way to notices, what if you're not ready to move on? Today gave me the chance to explore worship in a new way.

'So how did you come to join us today?' Dave asks.

I give a summary of Luke's tale, and Dave doesn't even register any interest in the 'gay vicar' side of the story. Quakers are inclusive after all. Dave's interest is piqued though in Luke's work as a prison chaplain.

'I visit prisoners from time to time – a few of us here do,' he says. 'You've heard of Elizabeth Fry?'

'Stephen's mum?' I guess.

Dave raises an eyebrow, then asks, 'Got a five pound note?'

'Oh I'm sorry,' I say. 'I thought the tea was free.'

'It was, you plonker,' Dave says with a laugh. Others turn to look. The word 'plonker' does not feature in Quaker liturgy. But then, nothing does.

Movers and Quakers

Just good Friends ...

- **Elizabeth Fry**: A social reformer known as 'the angel of prisons'. Also responsible for making treatment of prisoners more humane, and was the first woman to present evidence in Parliament. She remains captive, but comfortable, on the back of a five pound note.
- **Joseph Fry**: Founder of Fry's Chocolate and responsible for the first chocolate bar for mass production. Also responsible for Britain's first Easter Egg, unless you're under eight, in which case a) it's definitely the Easter Bunny, and b) well done reading this book.
- **John Cadbury**: A Quaker who didn't want to become a soldier or lawyer for religious reasons, so went into business making chocolate. His ethics made him campaign against animal cruelty, and he founded the precursor to the RSPCA. What he'd have made of Dairy Milk's ad campaign with a gorilla drumming to Phil Collins' 'In the Air Tonight', is anyone's guess. Today Cadbury's is known worldwide, and there are even Chinese Wispas, although when you buy one you have to pass the message down a line of people until they misunderstand what you originally asked for.
- **James Barclay**: One of the founders of Barclays Bank, who among other things gave us the world's first ATM machine in 1967, plus sent a variety of letters in red typeset to one Paul Kerensa from the year 1996 onwards.
- **Joseph Rowntree**: father of the founder of Rowntree's confectionary, promoter of education for York's poor community, and co-founder of life insurance company Friends Provident, the first to provide ethical investment funds.
- **Cyrus & James Clark**: founders of Clarks shoes. Quaker ethos meant they provided their workers with education, as well as housing on the condition they were kept alcohol-free. They also ran a tanning company – tanning hides that is, not

the faces of Liverpudlian women as the tanning trade has become.

From those peaceful early Quaker meetings came businesses worth billions. Silence is clearly golden.

I left the Meeting House, to ready myself for the big TV debut ...

The day of RX3 – Series C – Show: ~~'Miranda'~~ 'Kerensa' (title subject to renaming approval)

0845: My car arrives for door-to-door transfer. The driver offers me a choice of newspapers. He doesn't have what I'd like, but I don't make him pull in to a newsagent, nor do I make him wear the hat I've brought him.

0920: Arrive at TV Centre, escorted to dressing room. Flowers adorn the room, eventually, when I've unpacked them all. Spend several minutes turning the light bulbs around the mirror off and on. Blow a fuse.

1030: On set to walk through my first scene. All right, my only scene. I may have built up the part a little. I explore the set – smaller than I thought it would be, with doors from one room opening into another, and each piece of set littered with markings of shows it was used on previously. Some of these bits of wood have been in so many familiar shows, they deserve their own page on the IMDB. If walls could talk, that would make a great chat show.

I meet the cast, and they quickly put me at ease. They're a core team but go out of their way to make newcomers welcome.

The rehearsal for my big entrance comes and the floor manager walks me through where to stand and when. I've got marks to hit, props to carry and lines to listen out for. As for my own lines, I don't get a single one wrong. It was nothing, really. No really, don't applaud. The thing is, I have no lines.

The silent Quaker meeting was great practice, it turns out. You could say I was practising my lines throughout.

1400: Costume. It's my own costume, my everyday clothes. All right, the glamour's fading.

1630: Dress rehearsal. After five and a half hours of practising walking through a door, stopping, then walking some more, I think I've finally nailed it. Until we try it on set and it takes me three goes to get right. It turns out saying nothing and attempting to just walk is surprisingly difficult. It's practically choreography.

I've never excelled at the basic dramatic art of 'movement'. At drama school, we were divided into three sets depending on our foot coordination. The A group were formidable dancers, the B group were pretty nifty, and the C group were mostly hopeless. We were called in groups to try out for each set, and after I simply walked into the room, before even attempting a dance, the teachers decided that we needed a new D group.

1645: Back to dressing room. Sit. Wait.

This may be my first time in front of camera but I've been to enough of these recordings behind camera, and the days can be long. They bear a similarity to going to hospital for surgery: you know something good will come out of it, but in the meantime you're called in early and there's lots of waiting around. You'll end up in a windowless room for several hours, knowing it's in the hands of the experts but still unbearably nervous, hoping no one slips and damages the funny bone.

1700: Bored, nervous, I wander the corridor and bump into the comedian who'll warm up the studio audience. He doesn't recognise me out of writer's clothes, which is odd, because I'm wearing my writer's clothes, i.e. my clothes.

I explain that I've begged my way into a walk-on part, thanks to three years of writing for the show. How difficult can it be to walk on and say nothing? Very difficult, I've discovered.

1830: Make-up. Necessary, because everyone looks washed out and gaunt after eating in the BBC canteen under studio lights. I'm a little let down that it's not like when I was in school plays, in that I'm not painted orange. For some reason, in every production from *The Nativity* to *West Side Story*, I was cast as an Oompa Loompa.

The wardrobe team check over my outfit. They're seasoned pros, and always worth talking to for tales of when they worked on everything from *Blackadder* to *Black Books*. In fact, since entering the studio today, I've met crew who've worked on *Red Dwarf, The League of Gentlemen, Porridge* and *Fawlty Towers*. Even the wooden flats have made appearances in *Ab Fab* and *Dibley*, and this very studio was home to *Sykes, Dinnerladies, Only Fools and Horses, Morecambe & Wise* and *The Two Ronnies*.

Incredibly, we're told that this sitcom will be the last filmed in this studio. What a dynasty of comedy royalty. It's a humbling heritage, and I for one will miss these studios when they're converted into one big Ikea. Hopefully they'll save a blue plaque for it.

1930: Showtime. My big moment is nearly here, and all right it may not elevate me to McIntyrean levels. I'll still shop at Poundland, and may occasionally have a sponge cake meal on a whim. I won't let fame spoil me, largely because there won't be any fame.

My role may only be 'Customer', but I give it everything I've got. Oh you may think it small, but a part described as 'Taxi Driver' can mean a starring role for De Niro, and didn't *Braveheart* start out as 'Third Soldier from Left'?

Okay I admit 'Customer' – or 'Hank' as I've decided he's called, for the CV – isn't exactly a pivotal role. Bizarrely these few short seconds would I'm sure garner more recognition than the many combined days I've spent over the last few years writing lines for this same show. But then that's because as a writer, I'm a backroom boy. As a stand-up though, I'm a big show-off.

2030: My scene. I enter the studio, feeling the buzz of the studio audience instantly. They're not like an audience I'm used to – this is more like a convention. They're a little scary, not to mention the millions of unseen audience members who'll watch at home. If you thought about it too much, you'd go mad.

I await my cue, and it goes without saying, that I go, without saying, any words. I don't mess up my no lines by suddenly speaking or anything, but I'm still sure I've hit the wrong mark on the wrong line at the wrong moment. I'm only 90% sure I'm on the right set, but there's a camera with a red light on so I'm probably in roughly the right place.

We do it twice, for safety. It's not like the old days when they'd record *Dad's Army* in forty minutes, or maybe forty-five if they had to film a bomb detonating in a field. Some *Last of the Summer Wines* took less time to film than it did to watch them, thanks to using five different angles to film a bathtub of men descending a hill. Fact.[5]

2230: Post-show drinks. A chance to stand near famous people and nearly say something.

0000: Home, to sleeping wife and child.

I've not hit the big time: just brushed past it and given it a tap on the shoulder, and it told me it was busy and I should come back later. So I'll continue to traverse the country, write out of service stations, and hop from comedy club to comedy club to church. I'd have it no other way of course. I'm a stand-up bedouin, and life on the road suits me. Otherwise I'd have a mooing satnav for nothing.

That said, at the time of writing, the sitcom cameo to end all sitcom cameos has yet to be broadcast. By the time of publication, it will have been. So you, dear reader, know something I don't. My scene may have ended up on the cutting-room floor, in which case the above is a bittersweet tale of a missed opportunity. Or it may have been broadcast and be awful, in which case the above is an unfortunate tale of a should-have-been-missed opportunity. Or as I'm sure will be the case, the spin-off series could be in the pipeline – the *Frasier* to *Miranda*'s *Cheers*. '*Customer Who Enters Shop*'. Now that's a title with a ring to it.

[5] Not fact.

When I Surveyed the Wondrous Cross-Section of UK Christianity

Numbers are down, innovation is difficult to find, and invariably there's some over-casual middle-class man trying to keep the attention of a half-full room of starers. Comedy circuit or church? The accusation's been put to both. Yet, in my travels I've found that while both can contain this stereotype, if you seek it out, you'll find growing numbers, creativity, and involving, dynamic people fronting these rooms of joy.

Hopefully the previous 176 pages[1] have given a snapshot of both stand-up and kneel-down circuits. Both have evolved from, 'If you don't like the exact way we do it, tough – you can watch *Songs of Praise/Live at the Apollo* at home'. Certainly among Christians, evolution hasn't always come naturally.

Nowadays if you have a vague sense of humour, there'll be live comedy for you: from the bombastic chains of Jongleurs and Highlight, to the edgier independent nights in venues like Brighton's Komedia and Sheffield's Last Laugh, to the arts centres and live tours of cerebral Radio 4 stars or low-key comedy-music acts. Comedy now even fills stadia and arenae,[2] yet often the same acts are performing in a local comedy cellar in front of forty people for a quarter of the ticket price.

[1] So Amazon.com reports – impressive they know the page count, given I'm still writing this.
[2] I'm told 'stadiums' and 'arenas' are both acceptable words, but if you can't Latinly[3] pluralise in a book about churches, when can you?
[3] I know 'Latinly' is not an acceptable word. And that it's not the done thing to do footnotes on your footnotes. Sorry.

You can choose your comedy-going, and there's something for everyone.

Equally if you have a vague sense of a Christian soul, there will be a church for you. Every TV show seems to depict the same centuries-old stained-glass Anglican church, with a cassocked vicar and maybe a *Dad's Army* verger and a *Vicar of Dibley* committee. The truth is that there are small churches, big churches and mega-churches, meeting in theatres and cinemas and cafés and pubs. Some churches even meet in churches. There are traditionalists and forward-thinkers, lovers of ritual and armies of activists.

In this book I've endeavoured to represent both comedy and Christianity fairly, and to help with the latter, I set up an online survey about church life. I must thank the 268 respondents, who were frank about their own church experiences: encouraging and uplifting, as well as occasionally airing a few concerns. Their help was invaluable. If I may focus a little more on the churchy side than the comedy side to sum up, here's some of what they said ...

> 49% attend Anglican churches
> 30% are Evangelical
> 21% are Charismatic
> 18% go to Baptist churches
> 16% are Methodist
> 7% class themselves Pentecostal
> 4% are Roman Catholic

Some commented that divisions in the church were too great: 'There's too much fear and prejudice between Christian denominations,' said one person. 'We need greater understanding of different styles of connecting with God.' There are many ways to the mountain top, it seems. Others observed that too much is made of the differences: 'They're becoming less and less important.' 'Most Christians just get on with it,' said another. The point that 'Thinking differently is good and valuable,' was made by a dozen or so people, ironically.

Lines will always be drawn somewhere though: Roman Catholics don't permit Protestants to partake in communion, and groups such as Christian Scientists and Jehovah's Witnesses veer significantly from the mainstream. I once dated a Christian Spiritualist, who saw herself and her church as Christian – it's even in the name. For me, it had drifted too far. This wasn't dog collars versus open-neck shirts, like the distinction between some churches. Somewhere around the idea of Ouija boards at a Sunday service, my mental barriers went up.

But divisions wound us. Throughout this book, I've spoken about different forms of Christianity, but we shouldn't dwell on these differences. All they represent is that we are human, we are diverse, and as we gather together, different expressions of worship will emerge.

Resultantly, respondents spoke of great differences in worship and presentation styles. A third used Gifts of the Spirit, such as speaking in tongues. But one commented: 'Spiritual gifts are a hot potato: they're talked about, taught about, sometimes used, but rarely encouraged.' Two-thirds didn't think spontaneity was encouraged in services. Delightfully, very few found services either long or boring – and it was an anonymous survey so they could have said so if they thought it.[4]

Descriptions of church ranged from 'growing church plants'[5] to High Anglican 'bells and smells', via 'Anglo-Catholic mixed with Charismatic Evangelical', 'Post-evangelical' and even the baffling 'Revangelical', which must either mean that it's evangelical *again*, or that it's a spelling mistake. Some were part of 'church without walls': groups in cafés, or a market traders' church, or what one described as 'radical panto-style'.[6]

Traditional worship is still very popular, and many attend for the ritual. One said that her new church lacked regular Holy Communion, which made her realise its importance to her. It was argued too that many at home in 'traditional' churches (with an orthodox liturgy, and cathedral-style music) want to be socially inclusive. Those who want women bishops and gay priests shouldn't seek them only in new-builds; old-fashioned style doesn't mean old-fashioned values.

One woman spoke of her church becoming more – and too – traditional. Tradition is not something you only move away from, but something you can move towards and aspire to have, or avoid. The pitfalls of tradition were apparent too: one commented that Christianity

---

[4] Although I suppose God is always watching.

[5] Church plants are not like house plants but in a church; they're offshoots of a church planted elsewhere across town. A bit like a spider plant. Which is, confusingly, a house plant.

[6] I can only assume 'panto-style' church features organists creeping behind vicars ('He's behind you!') and worship lyrics being pointed to with a big stick. The response to, 'The peace of the Lord be with you,' changes from, 'And also with you,' to, 'Oh no it isn't.'

could be let down by ritualistic 'Sunday-only Christians'. Refreshingly 71% of respondents agreed that 'church' happens on Monday to Saturday, more than on Sundays. Yet Sundays were still seen as sacred: 'I'd like "Happy Sunday" to become a regular expression, like "Happy Christmas",' said one surveyee.

76% thought their church focused strongly on biblical teaching, while 19% felt it not to be a priority, with a further 5% who said the Bible was barely taught at all. The statistics were similar for sung worship and prayer. Most said that instead, the emphases of their churches were on serving the local community and welcoming newcomers. It meant that half felt church wasn't challenging enough, but there was a real sense that local church should be a hub of help. Some said we could go further: 'We're too concerned with "style of worship" or the colour of the floor. We need to be serving the community around us.'

A major frustration was the division between change-resisters in church and those seeking to move forward and attract youth, or those put off by tradition. 'We need to get over the gay thing', was a common comment. One said, 'I know several people (gay and straight) who wouldn't set foot near a church now, and that's not good,' and another admitted that homophobes in the church often made them embarrassed to be a Christian. 73% wanted the focus of their church to be on inclusivity rather than on judgement, while 9% preferred the other way round.

Many expressed keen interest in taking church *to* people rather than expecting them to walk through ancient doors, expressed by one replier: 'Get out of the building and show His love.' Yet one woman (who only attended her traditional church because her husband worked there) was frustrated that attempts to try alternative forms of church were 'fragile' and 'regarded as dodgy' by the mainline church. Another enjoyed the 'varied styles of worship found at events such as Greenbelt', but found them so rarely at Sunday services that they attended 'more out of obligation than enthusiasm', until the more alternative forms of worship find a place in the four walls of a church.

I asked what would make a perfect church, and many – even most – replied saying there was no such thing on this earth, although three said a perfect church should be messy, with cake. Church is imperfect, because we are: 'That's why I fit in so well,' explained one punter. Groucho Marx said that he wouldn't belong to any club that would have him as a member. Hopefully those who think the same about churches will come anyway. 48% of repliers said their churches gain new people all the time, so despite the media's impression, UK church looks in rude health. With a little movement on alternative forms of worship and greater social inclusion, that health will only get, er, ruder.

For my part, I love the diversity of the church, from Rogators to Quakers to Candlestick Catholics, just as I love the variety of the comedy circuit, whether cruise shows, fringe shows or cringe shows. There is no such thing as the perfect venue, the perfect gig or the perfect church. Perfection may be beautiful, but imperfection is pretty darn appealing.

I'm aware that I haven't given the punchline yet, of this book. So a comedian walks into a church ...

Well, like the saying goes, always leave the audience wanting m